Wings
on the
Water

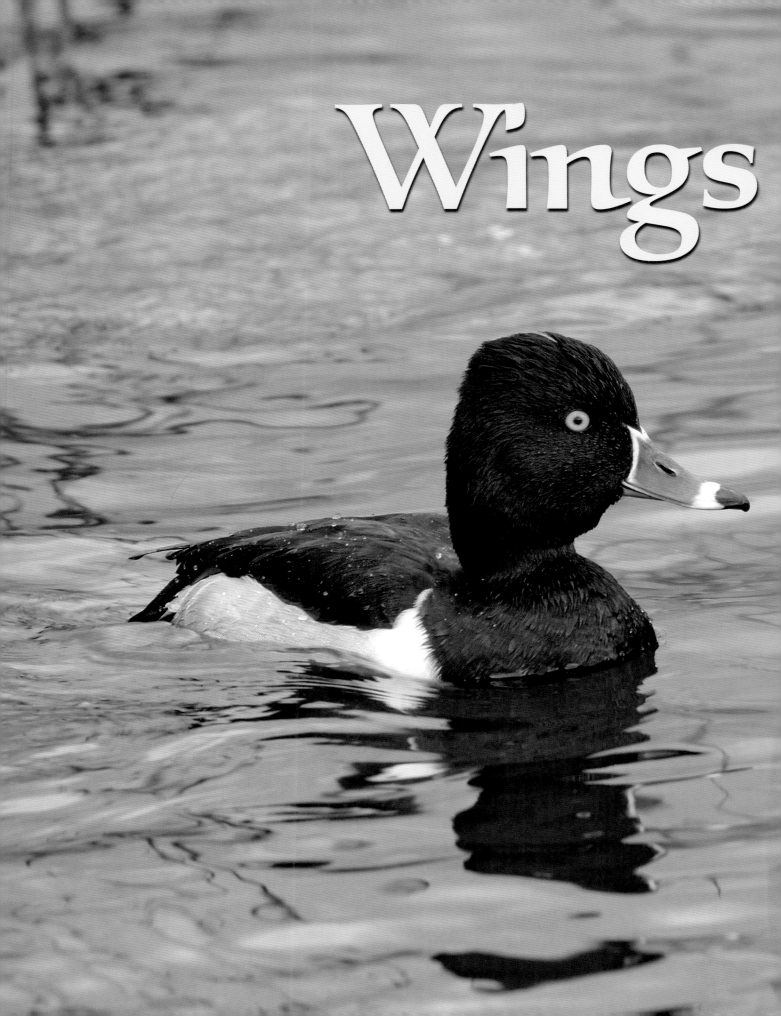

Wings

on the Water

The Great Gallery of Ducks, Geese, and Loons

PHOTOGRAPHY BY STEVE MASLOWSKI

STACKPOLE
BOOKS

Published by
STACKPOLE BOOKS
5067 Ritter Road
Mechanicsburg, PA 17055
www.stackpolebooks.com

Customer Service (877) 462-2604
www.wildfowl-carving.com

Printed in China

10 9 8 7 6 5 4 3 2 1

Library of Congress Cataloging-in-Publication Data

Maslowski, Stephen.
     Wings on the water : the great gallery of ducks, geese, and loons / photography
  by Steve Maslowski. — 1st ed.
       p.   cm.
     ISBN 978-1-881982-84-5 (hardcover)
     1. Ducks—Pictorial works. 2. Geese—Pictorial works. 3. Loons—Pictorial
works. 4. Photography of birds. I. Title.
QL696.A52M357 2012
598.4'1—dc23
                                                                    2011045646

Contents

Preface

Wildfowl Carving Magazine has been around since 1985. Over those years one of the magazine's staples has been reference articles about all kinds of birds—turkeys, eagles, sparrows, cardinals, jays, blackbirds, and woodcock among them.

But in the end it seems always to come back to ducks.

In fact, we can thank ducks for the entire art form we call wildfowl carving. It all started with decoys, duck facsimiles that hunters used to lure unwitting waterfowl within range of their guns. Whether the decoys were crude or well-crafted, their original purpose was a practical one—meat for the table.

Over the years carvers began carving birds for decorative purposes. Many of these carvings still portrayed ducks, but these works were aimed at the shelf or mantelpiece instead of a spot in front of a duck blind. Eventually carvers began creating lifelike renditions of all kinds of birds—and we display the amazing diversity of wildfowl carving in *Competition*, our annual showcase of the best work from shows across the United States and Canada. But just as we can trace birds back to the dinosaurs, we find that even the most intricate and lifelike bird carving has duck decoys at the base of its family tree.

One thing on which all carvers can agree is that reference material is important to the carving process. If you want to capture a sense of realism in wood you need to know what the real thing looks like. Check out the very first issue of *Wildfowl Carving Magazine* (Spring 1985) and you'll find a reference article by Frank Bellrose about the wood duck. (That article appears in this volume, starting on page 194). Carvers obviously consult photographs so they can get things to look right, but the words in these articles help as well. They give carvers a better overall sense of what the birds are like. A picture may be worth a thousand words—but the words lead to a greater understanding of a species and its behaviors and help carvers capture its essence.

To create this book we went back over that quarter-century of *Wildfowl Carving* and collected all the duck articles—as well as a few about geese, loons, and other waterfowl. We've been very fortunate over the years to rely on the talents of some great nature writers, as you'll discover within these pages. And then we asked Steve Maslowski, who has been providing wildlife photography (and words, too!) to the magazine for years, if he would supply us with new photos for this book. That's what he did and the images he took capture these beautiful birds in their natural settings. The word "breathtaking" springs to mind.

You don't have to be a carver to appreciate the birds in this book, though. Hunters, birders, and nature lovers will find plenty to enjoy here. The photographs are beautiful and the species they illustrate are captivating. As you look through them you might find yourself being transported to the rivers, lakes, and streams where these striking birds congregate. We hope that maybe *Wings on the Water* will help you to a new appreciation of nature's handiworks. Enjoy!

Tom Huntington
Editor, *Wildfowl Carving Magazine*
and *Competition*

Introduction

BY STEVE MASLOWKSI

I went on my first duck hunt when I was about 12 years old. I accompanied my father and one of his favorite duck-hunting companions on a December weekend excursion to Paducah, Kentucky, not far from the confluence of the Ohio River and the mighty Mississippi. Vast, soggy bottomlands stretched for miles and I could see scudding clouds of ducks flying every which way in the gray winter light. They provided a remarkable distraction from the cold wind that chilled my young bones. I don't remember how many ducks flew close enough for me to swing my little 20-gauge in their direction, but I shot a lot and missed every time. The weekend left me more than a little dismayed. How could anybody hit those jet birds with after-burners? "With luck" has been my answer ever since.

The difficulty of hitting a flying duck really hit home when I started photographing them. A bird that approaches you from the side for a flyby at about 25 yards seems to be moving slowly when still at a distance. "Duck soup," you think as the bird gradually grows in size in the viewfinder. But once the duck gets into good range it suddenly seems to accelerate. Suddenly it's a 40-mph missile, forcing the photographer to pivot the long and heavy telephoto lens as fast as possible, and sometimes even faster. When the duck flies away along its foreshortened angle it seems to slow down again, adding a final insult to the photographer, who missed the perfect shot by a mile.

All this is a long way of saying that while photographing for this book I spent an inordinate amount of time trying to get flight shots, and fell woefully short of ever getting my limit. But what fun I had!

Early in this project I made the decision to photograph mostly wild, free-flying birds so I could indulge in the passion many of us share—hunting. I may have been shooting with a camera instead of a gun but the wind remained just as cold. (And I ended up with about the same number of ducks for the dinner table). I finally visited zoos and the like for a few close-ups but otherwise the birds in this book were free flying, with wing feathers intact and in the habitats they picked themselves.

Of course I had a lot of firepower on my side. The evolution of camera gear over the four decades I've been photographing made it seem like I was shooting with the equivalent of a 10-gauge shotgun, not a little 20. In practical terms, though, a flying duck still has to be within shotgun range if I want to get a reasonable photograph.

Successful photography depends on the same principle as a successful hunt: Go where the birds are. That meant I had to range from New Mexico to Idaho, Florida to Maine, Maryland to California, and points in between. But where a hunter prefers birds that aren't overly "educated" and wary, the best ducks to photograph are those that have grown at least somewhat used to birdwatchers and other people. Tameness is a widespread phenomenon for mallards, but for wood ducks, ringnecks, goldeneyes and the like, it varies by locality. Some species, such as buffleheads and hooded mergansers, never seemed to relax or cooperate. As a wildlife biologist once told me about ring-necked pheasants, "You just can't tame 'em".

"Tame" or not, the free-flying ducks here are presented in all their glory. They still have their magically waterproof plumage, sturdy constitutions, and strong instincts that make them favor this body of water over that. I found them resting, preening, courting, feeding, flocking, and swimming to-and-fro as nature intended. And when they flew, it was fast.

Not every wildfowl carver will want to try carving a duck with its wings outstretched. *That* is a true challenge. But I think every woodworker and artist wants to catch the natural essence of the ducks and other waterbirds I've photographed for this volume. On one level you find their essence in the wariness and other patterns, their swiftness in flight, and their affinity for water and weather conditions that we might find brutal. On another, their essence flows from tens of thousands of years of evolutionary carving that has resulted in birds with specially refined shapes and meticulously detailed plumage that helps them cope—and thrive—in their habitat. While I certainly enjoyed the challenges of capturing the first essence, I've also tried in these photos to capture some of the wonder of the latter as well.

In any event, I thank the editors of *Wildfowl Carving Magazine* and Stackpole Books for giving me the excuse to spend many wonderful days hunting ducks and other waterfowl. Hopefully the harvest in these pages will help others satisfy their hunger to pay artistic homage to the world of waterfowl.

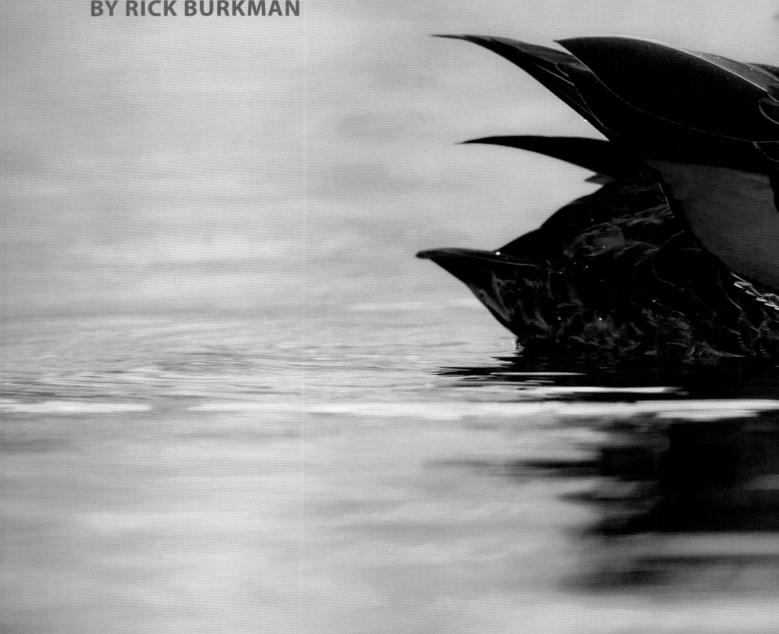

American Black Duck
(*Anas rubripes*)

BY RICK BURKMAN

Opening pages: Preening keeps the feathers oiled and able to repel water. Unlike the mallard, the black duck has black, not white, around the blue speculum. *Above:* A drake assumes a classic decoy pose. The subtleties of the duck's coloring can make it a challenge for carvers.

"Look what's coming to the feeder," my wife said to me as we were sipping our morning coffee. I looked out the window and, to my surprise, saw six ducks waddling up the snowy riverbank toward our pole-mounted bird feeder. There was one mallard drake, two mallard hens, and, most impressively, three dark brown handsome American black ducks (*Anas rubripes*).

I have watched ducks dive, dip, and walk through farm fields for food, but I never imagined I would see four-pound waddlers like these compete with the penny-weight birds that normally frequent our feeders. These ducks, however, found this treasure to their liking. They must have shared the good news, because during the course of the year we had as many as 25 wild mallards, black ducks, and black duck-mallard hybrids visiting our bird feeders. Some of the braver—or maybe just hungrier—ducks tried flying up to the feeder and grabbing the tiny perch meant for much smaller, non-webbed feet. They sprayed sunflower seeds on the ground, providing a feast for the birds waiting below. Gullets filled, the sated birds reclined in the snow and napped in the afternoon sunshine.

The raids on our feeders should not have been a surprise—like many wild creatures, ducks are opportunistic and they eat and thrive wherever they can find a bountiful harvest. And opportunity abounds when your diet includes an eclectic mix of leaves, seeds, roots, insects, snails, crabs, tad-

poles, and fish. Finding this abundance of food is generally easy for the gregarious black ducks, which live throughout the eastern states in any season as long as they can find enough open water to support their aquatic lifestyle.

PAIRING UP

Black ducks like variety, in their diet and in their love life. Although black ducks usually mate with other black ducks, hybridizations have occurred with northern pintails, American wigeons, mallards, mottled ducks, and even unusual species like the common pochard and Muscovy duck. Black ducks are members of the anatid family, which means they are closely related to many of these species. In fact, mottled ducks and black ducks are so similar that people considered them the same species, the dusky duck, until late in the nineteenth century.

But there is little doubt that black ducks, overall, prefer to mate with other black ducks. Courtship begins in late winter or early spring. When a male finds a suitable female he begins to show off. In an ancient dance driven by hormonal urges, he begins swimming in circles around his chosen mate. He may flatten his head and neck to the water and spread his wings to show off his iridescent speculum. This normally sociable bird now turns aggressive, driving other ducks away so they can't encroach on his territory. He lunges and attacks interlopers and chases them across the water in pursuit flights that can continue for up to a half mile.

Once the ducks have selected mates, they begin the important job of nest building. Black ducks like to nest near wetland habitats, and they are equally comfortable in bogs, lakes, marshes, ponds, and rivers. They don't place nests directly on or along the shores of water bodies or wetlands. Instead, black ducks move inland into nearby forests, shrublands, and other vegetated areas, sometimes up to 200 yards or more from the shoreline. Both the male and the female will help select the nest site, and some spots are so popular the ducks use them year after year. Although typically thought of as ground nesters, black ducks will also nest in old ravens' nests, eagle nests, tree cavities, and on top of old stumps. Ducks, like some other large game birds, often engage in a strange behavior known as egg dumping, when a female lays eggs in another bird's nest while the brooding mother is away. Sometimes it's in the nest of another black duck, but often it's the nest of another species.

Above right: This photo affords a nice view of the head and bill from the front. *Right:* Hens and drakes look very much alike. The one obvious difference is bill color. The male has a yellow bill, while the hen's is olive.

Black Duck Measurements*				
	Adult Male	**Adult Female**	**Immature Male**	**Immature Female**
Length	21.6–24.2 in. Average 22.5 in.	20.0–23.7 in. Average 20.8 in.	21.6–23.7 in. Average 22.4 in.	19.0–23.5 in. Average 20.0 in.
Wing	11.4 in.	10.7 in.	11.1 in.	10.4 in.
Weight	2.5–3.4 lbs. Average 2.76 lbs.	2.3–3.3 lbs. Average 2.45 lbs.	2.3–3.4 lbs. Average 2.64 lbs.	2.0–3.2 lbs. Average 2.39 lbs.

*Unless otherwise noted, information in the measurement charts throughout the book is from *Ducks, Geese and Swans of North America* by Frank C. Bellrose, 1980. Used with permission.

Facing page: The black duck is handsome, with deep brown body feathers bordered by lighter edges the color of softly-tanned suede.

Both parents may help with the site selection, but the female alone builds the nest. She pushes, scrapes, and shoves dirt and soil with her bill and feet until she forms a depression in the soil. She then pulls grasses, leaves, and small stems into the scrape and weaves them together, continually rearranging the nesting materials to fit her body. Feathers provide insulation and warmth. The nest is never really complete—even after laying her eggs the hen will continue to pull in nearby vegetation to shore up the sides, and she will pile grasses over the top of her body and nest to form a nest cavity.

Once the nest is ready the hen begins laying one egg a day until she has a clutch of nine or ten creamy white or pale greenish eggs. Then she waits. For the next 25 days she will warm and turn the eggs and protect them from raccoons, mink, snakes, foxes, crows, and any other creature that relishes a fresh egg meal.

A mother duck is patient—she not only sits for long periods on her clutch of eggs, but she will also sit tight when a predator approaches and often won't leave the nest until an intruder almost steps on her. Then, in a flurry of feathers, she will flush away from the nest and land a short distance away, often dragging one wing, pitifully slapping and flapping along like a mortally wounded bird and an easy meal. She leads the intruder farther and farther from her nest until she believes her charges are safe, and then she miraculously recovers and flies quickly away, quacking and scolding the startled intruder as she escapes to safety.

In time, the unborn ducklings start calling to each other through their shells. This is the signal that it is time for them to work their way out into the world. Each duckling uses the egg tooth at the top of its bill to puncture the shell 25 or 30 times. Then, with a little bit of force, it pops off the egg's end and emerges, looking wet and bedraggled. Once free of their shells the baby ducks spend a few hours drying, and then they're ready to follow their mom. She quietly clucks encouragement to the olive-brown-and-yellow hatchlings as they leave their woodland nest to become water-based creatures, looking like little more than brown balls of fluff on top of the water as they skitter behind the watchful hen.

Leaving the eggs exposes the ducklings to a threatening world. Even under the watchful care of a mother duck, life is dangerous for a little fluff ball that weighs no more than a penny. Snapping turtles, northern pike, and pickerel stalk the little birds from below the water's surface; gulls, ospreys, eagles, and terns eye the youngsters from the air. Cold

Some black ducks make a long, perilous journey to their wintering grounds, while other populations are comfort migrants, hopping from open water to open water throughout the winter months.

temperatures can lower their body temperatures and winds can buffet them, forcing the little birds to expend vital energy stores.

The young birds need to grow rapidly, so they begin feeding as soon as they start running around. The mother duck may protect and care for her young, but that maternal care does not extend to providing nourishment. Each newly hatched duckling must quickly learn which waterborne specks are food and which are fluff. Instinct along with trial and error quickly teach them to recognize caddis flies, mayflies, water beetles, snails, aquatic worms, and other invertebrates that populate their lake and river homes and make up the bulk of their forage. As the birds grow older and larger they add tadpoles, small frogs, minnows, grains, aquatic tubers, and leaves to their diets.

GROWING UP

The little birds turn into handsome young adults with deep brown body feathers bordered by lighter edges the color of softly-tanned suede. Their abdomens are lighter, fading from dark brown to a whitish color, and their bills and feet are a sharp contrast in orange. The whitish underwings sharply contrast with their overall dark body coloration. The speculum is violet-blue with little or no trailing white edge. (One way to differentiate the black duck from its close relative the mallard is by the speculum—the mallard has a light blue speculum bordered by white on the top and bottom edges).

As young birds grow to adulthood they join older birds to begin their annual migration. For some birds, migration is a long, perilous journey. Many black ducks, on the other hand, are comfort migrants—hopping from open water to open water, stopping in farm fields and ponds to roost and eat. Sometimes black ducks will form large rafts on larger bodies of water, where the birds will mill around, preen, and rest in preparation for their upcoming flight. Migration takes place at night, while rest and feeding take place during the daylight hours.

Some people think that the black duck is slowly disappearing. It readily interbreeds with the mallard and the mallard phenotype often shows through, resulting in a brown-bodied black duck with a green sheen on its head. Interbreeding is so common in some areas that ornithologists have suggested that the two birds are color variations of the same species. Yet, the distinctive nature, colors, and habits of each species persevere, and both black duck and mallard populations appear stable, if somewhat lower in numbers. Species dilution, although common, does not appear to be a death knell for the black duck at this time.

In an earlier century, market hunting dealt a devastating blow to the wild black duck populations. Hunters with enormous boat-mounted guns killed hundreds of rafting birds at a time. Market hunting was outlawed in the early 1900s and the species rebounded and began to thrive in many of its old haunts. Today the loss of wetlands and waterways decreases the available habitat for the black duck, probably the largest factor that limits its current population growth. Even so, the black duck remains a common sight on the waterways, a handsome waterfowl with a rich history and, sometimes, a penchant for robbing bird feeders.

Top: This drake has his head lowered, a common pose in hunting rigs. *Bottom:* The feathers on the abdomen are lighter than the rest of the body, and the orange feet and yellow bill are a sharp contrast with the overall dark body coloration.

Bufflehead
(Bucephala albeola)

BY DR. A. J. ERSKINE

A feeding flock of buffleheads is like an iceberg—nine-tenths of it is underwater at any given moment! Constant activity distinguishes the bufflehead from all other species of ducks, and its incessant busyness makes watching both males and females fascinating. Of all of its activities, diving is its trademark, and for that reason, hunters in the Northeast call the bufflehead "dipper." Out west, however, hunters call it "butterball" in recognition of its build—the size of a teal but chunkier.

The closest relatives of the bufflehead are the gold-eneyes, or "whistlers." As with its relatives, the bufflehead drake's breast and belly are white. The upper surface and wings are glossy black, with broad white wing areas including several secondaries (inner wing feathers) and their coverts, but the leading edges of the wings are blackish with faint white flecking. The rump is off-white; the tail,

Opening pages: These two young male buffleheads are off on an adventure! *Above:* A side view of an adult male reveals faint iridescence—greenish on the forehead, purplish on the cheek. *Left:* The white area of the wing extends across the secondaries and their coverts, and the leading edge of the wing has mottled black-and-white feathering. The underwings are also mottled black and white.

gray. The puffy black head bears a white patch (the "shawl") extending from the eye and cheek right around the nape and crown from one side to the other. Close up, in certain lights, the black of the head may show iridescent reflections of reddish through greenish to purplish, but in the water, the drake shows only black and white.

On the female the white is reduced to small areas on a few secondaries and on the sides of the head, and the breast and under-parts are off-white to "tattletale gray." The rest of her head, back, wings and tail are never as black as in the male, although the wings are often a dark charcoal-gray, especially in fall. Soon after the molt, all the dark areas fade through the winter and spring to varying shades of drab gray to brownish gray.

A HEAD START

Few species of ducks nest in tree cavities, with the wood duck the most familiar example of the small group of ducks that do. The bufflehead is the only species in that group small enough to nest in the unaltered cavities excavated by the common flicker. Other songbirds compete with buffleheads for nest cavities, but buffle-

Top: Note where the eye falls in the cheek patch. The color of the bill for both sexes is bluish-gray to black. *Bottom:* This bufflehead in flight shows off his wing and tail feathers to a carver's delight.

Bufflehead Measurements				
	Adult Male	**Adult Female**	**Immature Male**	**Immature Female**
Length	14–15.6 in. Average 14.75 in.	12.7–13.7 in. (all females) Average 13.12 in.	13.9–15.2 in. Average 14.50 in.	
Wing	6.68 in.	6.10 in.	6.53 in.	5.96 in.
Weight	0.88–1.4 lbs. Average 1.06 lbs.	0.68–1.26 lbs. Average 0.81 lb.	0.9–1.2 lbs. Average 1.08 lbs.	0.6–1.2 lbs. Average 0.75 lb.

Above left: The female has varying shades of plumage, darkest on the flight feathers of the wing and on the head, grading to brownish-gray on the sides and upper breast. *Left:* Young males are duller than adult males and may be mistaken for females, but have the blue-gray bill and will gradually brighten in color to their full adult plumage. *Above right:* Buffleheads must make a running start to take wing.

heads start nesting earlier in the year than most species, which gives them a head start. Sometimes, though, their nests are taken over by starlings or bluebirds during the two-week period when the female is in the nest only to lay her eggs.

Buffleheads lay six to eleven eggs, most commonly nine eggs. As in all ducks, the female alone incubates for about 30 days. Nesting success is high, with 92 percent of the eggs in successful nests hatching. Failures still do occur, however. If disturbances happen during laying, the eggs may be abandoned.

The black-and-white downy young leave the nest by leaping to the ground 24–28 hours after hatching, and the female leads them to the nearest water. At that stage, the small size of buffleheads becomes a liability, as the tiny (23 g) ducklings may be lost on the way to water more easily than the larger chicks of other ducks. The young fledge on permanent ponds and sloughs in which emergent vegetation is mostly restricted to the shore-lines. Breeding seldom occurs on lakes and river systems where northern pike live; this large fish preys upon small ducklings.

From this view, you can count the tail feathers and note the pinkish webbed feet of the bufflehead.

The young birds grow rapidly and make their first flights seven to eight weeks after reaching the water. Meanwhile, the adults and yearlings have begun molting, as all the large flight feathers of wings and tail are replaced in late summer. A flightless period lasting three to four weeks follows the shedding of old feathers. When the new feathers grow enough to support flight, buffleheads begin flying again, usually by mid-September They do not start migrating, though, until mid-October. In the meantime they complete the body molt. Males return to the familiar black-and-white plumage that had been shed in the "eclipse" of early summer, when an inconspicuous appearance was an advantage during the flightless period. Migration to wintering areas occurs between mid-October and early December. Buffleheads winter along both coasts.

In this straight-on view of the head, you can see the details of the eye placement, cheek patch, iridescence, and bill.

UPWARDS-STRETCH-AND-WING-FLAP

Buffleheads remain on wintering areas for up to six months (October to April), and their everyday life, social behavior and postures may be most readily studied then. Like all ducks, buffleheads spend some time each day in preening, which leads to some oddly contorted attitudes as the birds stretch "over the shoulder" to reach the back plumage or roll over almost upside-down to preen the belly feathers. Most sessions of preening end with the "upwards-stretch-and-wing-flap" sequence (also seen in several other species of ducks); that action is also seen, in ritualized form, at the ends of many social interaction sequences involving buffleheads.

The most frequently seen and characteristic interactive poses include the "head-forward-threat," a slightly crouched posture with sleeked plumage, that is recognized as a threat to attack; the "fly-over-and-landing" of a male showing off his bright pink feet for the female he is courting; and the "head-bobbing" that follows the ritualized fly-over/landing/wing-flick sequence.

When you go out to observe buffleheads, pick an area of shore in a bay or lagoon rather than on the open coast, as these birds lead sheltered lives compared to the larger diving ducks. Often it is possible to watch, from a parked car on a shoreline road or in a park, buffleheads "doing their thing" close to shore. Brief periods of preening or loafing punctuate the buffleheads' main activity: diving, over and over and over again, as the dipper lives up to its nickname.

Canvasback
(*Aythya valisineria*)

BY G. MICHAEL HARAMIS

Opening pages: The canvasback is a regal-looking bird as it floats gracefully upon the water. *Above:* Displaying classic landing form, this canvasback places his feet beneath his body and uses them like skis.

I vividly remember my first encounter with canvasbacks. It was early January in the Finger Lakes country of western New York, one of those gray winter days with the wind slanting fine snow across Cayuga Lake. Visibility was about 200 yards, the wind gusting from the north. I was bird watching along the beach, binoculars in hand, periodically searching open water for a glimpse of a goldeneye, horned grebe, or if more fortunate, a common loon tracking on the waves. Suddenly, a loose V of about a dozen waterfowl burst into view like a squadron of miniature jet fighters; before I could lift my glasses they had passed south along the shoreline and had disappeared in a snowy blur. The speed and directness of their flight was powerful, impressive. The long necks and wedge-shaped bills were unmistakable field marks of our most famous North American duck—the canvasback.

SPECIES PROFILE

The canvasback (*Aythya valisineria*) is one of 35 indigenous species of waterfowl in North America and is the largest of 14 closely related species of diving ducks worldwide called pochards or, more commonly, bay ducks. The canvasback slightly exceeds the mallard (*Anas platyrhynchos*) and the American black duck (*A. rubripes*) as the largest inland duck in North America (excluding sea ducks). As a research biologist for the U.S. Fish and Wildlife Service, I have weighed thousands of canvasbacks during trapping and band operations on the Chesapeake Bay and have found December weights of adult male canvasbacks to average about 3 pounds, with the heaviest individuals approaching 3.75 pounds. In comparison, adult females and juvenile males average about 2.8 pounds and juvenile females are lightest at 2.6 pounds.

Top and bottom: The female displays a pattern of plumage similar to the male's, in subtle shades of brown.

The canvasback was first described by the famous American ornithologist Alexander Wilson in his *American Ornithology*, published in several volumes between 1808 and 1814. The species apparently was overlooked by earlier naturalists because of its similarity to the common pochard (*Aythya ferina*) of Eurasia, a species with which European immigrants were likely familiar. The canvasback is closest to the common pochard in appearance and overall biology, although in North America the canvasback is most similar to and at a distance sometimes confused with the redhead. Close at hand the differences between the two species are readily apparent, as a quick glance at any good bird guide can verify. The most outstanding difference between the two species is the distinctive wedge-shaped head and bill profile of the canvasback versus the rounded head profile of the redhead. This feature and the greater darkness of redheads of both sexes over their canvasback counterparts (male redheads are gray-backed birds while canvasbacks are white-backed) help separate the two species when viewed at great distance.

FOODS AND RANGE

Canvasbacks feed on a variety of plant and animal foods throughout the annual cycle, but greatly prefer plant

Canvasback Measurements				
	Adult Male	**Adult Female**	**Immature Male**	**Immature Female**
Length	20.0–21.9 in. Average 20.73 in.	18.8–20.4 in. Average 19.81 in.	19.8–21.2 in. Average 20.48 in.	19.2–20.1 in. Average 19.67 in.
Wing	10.39 in.	9.01 in.	9.09 in.	8.75 in.
Weight	1.9–3.5 lbs. Average 2.76 lbs.	2.0–3.4 lbs. Average 2.55 lbs.	2.3–3.3 lbs. Average 2.75 lbs.	2.1–3.1 lbs. Average 2.53 lbs.

Top: Here is a nice rear view of the drake. *Bottom:* A classic profile view of the drake.

In the 1800s, Wilson recognized the importance of wild celery in the diet of the canvasback stating "wherever this plant grows in abundance, the canvasback may be expected either to pay occasional visits or to make it their regular residence during winter . . . while in waters unprovided with this nutritive plant, they are altogether unknown." So important was wild celery in this region that Wilson chose *valisineria* as the canvasback's species-specific name.

Canvasbacks breed in the interior of the continent and formerly were well distributed throughout the central prairie region north to the parklands of Canada. Some breed in intermountain regions north to central Alaska (Fort Yukon), northern MacKenzie and Great Slave Lake. Because prairie breeding habitats in the contiguous United States, especially Minnesota and the Dakotas, have been greatly reduced by the spread of grain agriculture and the associated drainage of wetlands, most canvasbacks breed in the prairie provinces of Canada. Canvasbacks achieve their greatest breeding density in the glaciated pothole country of southwestern Manitoba where a complex of numerous large and small wetlands of varying permanence exists. Under excellent May water conditions, each square mile of this habitat may contain 80 or more wetlands.

Locally throughout its range the canvasback has been known by many names including "white-back," "sheldrake," "bullneck," "can," "canard cheval," "gray duck," "hickory-quaker," and "red-headed bullneck." The name canvasback is believed to have been in use since at least 1800 and probably originated in the upper Chesapeake Bay region. The name is believed to refer to the delicately vermiculated white body plumage of the male that resembles canvas fabric. It has also been speculated that the name may have originated from the

foods during the non-breeding period. They are especially fond of submersed aquatic plants and prefer tubers, rootstalks, and winter buds over other plant parts. Although canvasbacks compete with other ducks for a variety of aquatic foods, they possess the unique ability to probe in bottom sediments with their long wedge-shaped bills to extract food items. This forag-

ing technique permits canvasbacks almost sole use of subterranean plant foods and burrowing animals including small clams, worms, and a variety of insect larvae. Sago pondweed (*Potamogeton pectinatus*), duck potato (*Sagittaria latifolia*), and wild celery (*Vallisneria americana*) are especially important during fall migration and early winter.

Powerful breast muscles, used for flight, give the canvasback a somewhat chunky appearance. Because of this form, cans tend to float lower in the water than dabbling ducks.

practice of transporting market hunted birds in canvas bags which were labeled "canvas—back" to indicate their return for reuse.

DIVING AND FLYING

Like all pochards, canvasbacks are well adapted for diving. They have short, narrow wings and scapulars to reduce drag and buoyancy, while their large webbed feet, placed well back on the body, facilitate swimming underwater. Because of reduced wing area and, therefore, lift characteristics, canvasbacks must employ more rapid and powerful wingbeats and achieve higher speeds to attain flight than comparably sized dabbling ducks like the mallard or the black duck. To power their wings, canvasbacks have large, dense breast muscles that give them a compact chunky appearance. This compact form is in part why canvasbacks and other pochards float somewhat lower in the water in comparison to dabbling ducks.

Because of their high-speed flight characteristics, canvasbacks have difficulty maneuvering at low speeds or in tight places. Landings and takeoffs require considerable space and exclude canvasbacks from using the very small wetlands or landing on land. Landings are made at considerable speed and canvasbacks must use broad, wide turns and brake abruptly using their webbed feet placed beneath the body, like skis, to contact the water. On takeoff, canvasbacks use a running start and full wing power to gain enough speed for liftoff. The birds use every advantage of headwind—which can make the maneuver effortless. However, in absence of such assistance they often must labor 20 to 30 feet before clearing the water.

COURTSHIP AND MATING

Unlike dabbling ducks, which begin pairing in the fall, canvasback courtship begins on the wintering ground with the arrival of spring temperatures in late February and March.

Large flocks amass for migration and courtship begins in earnest. On calm, warm days, the air is filled with male courtship notes that accompany head-throw and kinked-neck displays. At such times entire flocks may be comprised of small courtship parties of several males pursuing one or more females. These parties become more obvious as males push close to a female and perform the neck-stretch display.

Courtship continues throughout migration and most birds arrive paired on the breeding ground. Females usually begin nesting in early May and prefer cattail, bulrush, or white-top marsh grass cover for nest sites. Courtship and other social activity occur on larger potholes while females select smaller isolated wetlands to build nests. Nests are built over water and although large, are well-camouflaged. The average clutch size is eight to ten eggs; however wide-

The canvasback drake's head is rusty-red and his bill is black, but it is his red eye that really captures your attention.

The hen and drake's distinctive vermiculation, which resembles canvas fabric, may have provided the inspiration for this beautiful waterfowl's name.

spread parasitism by redheads commonly reduces the number of canvasback eggs incubated and, subsequently, young produced. Redheads are specialists at laying eggs in canvasback nests before nesting on their own.

Water permanence is crucial to breeding success—declining water levels can lead to nest desertion or catastrophic predation of nests or young by mink, raccoon, and fox. During drought, canvasbacks may seek better nesting habitats or simply forgo nesting. Good water conditions foster high brood survival by providing abundant food and reducing the number of overland movements required of flightless broods.

Males desert females early in the incubation period and move to large lakes to undergo molt. As with all ducks, geese, and swans, canvasbacks molt all their flight feathers at once and become flightless for a period of about a month. During this time, they depend on permanent water to supply food and safety from predators.

Canvasbacks begin migration into the northern Great Plains in September with peak migration movement occurring in October. They are cold-hardy ducks and many defer migration until the threat of freeze-up. Primary mi-

gration routes are east through the Great Lakes region to the Chesapeake Bay and the Atlantic Coast. Canvasbacks also migrate along the Pacific Flyway and winter in San Francisco Bay. Canvasbacks rarely winter in marine environments but prefer coastal brackish waters. Some birds migrate as far south as Mexico, where they winter on interior freshwater lakes.

As one of the most highly prized quarry of wildfowlers since colonial times, it is not surprising that the canvasback occupies a special place in the history of decoy craft and as a subject of modern decoy art. Probably nowhere else was the craft of the working decoy so diversified as in the Chesapeake Bay region where canvasback hunting had its longest period of development. For up until a few decades ago, hunting of wildfowl in this region meant hunting canvasbacks. Perhaps in this light it is even more fitting that the canvasback is subject of the earliest known decoy in North America. Twelve decoys, hand crafted from tule reeds by ancient Paiute peoples and estimated to be over 1,000 years old were removed from Lovelock Cave, Nevada, in 1924. These decoys were celebrated as the subject of the first Nevada duck stamp in 1979.

Eiders
(Common, King, Steller's, and Spectacled)

(Somateria mollissima, Somateria spectabilis, Polysticta stelleri, Somateria fischeri)

BY STEVE MASLOWSKI

Opening pages: The king eider manages to maintain his royal demeanor even while bathing. *Above:* This common eider shows an uncommon rear view of his wings outstretched and the back of his head.

Few ducks seem as rugged as eiders. They thrive in the mercilessly cold, windy salt waters that rim the roof of the continent. There they endure temperatures as cold as minus 50 degrees Fahrenheit, fly through blinding fog and blizzards, and bob near ice packs and rocky shores upon which 75-knot winds heave mountainous, crashing waves. Through it all, they seem impervious to these elements that are capable of snatching a human's life in minutes. Eiders are indeed blessed with some of the world's best natural insulation.

Four species of eider occur in North America: common, king, Steller's, and spectacled; only two of these commonly venture as far south as the northeastern United States. Not surprisingly, few people have seen all four species.

To those fortunate enough to see them, adult male eiders present memorable images. They stand out from the crowd with their large, handsome, black-and-white designs. Upon closer inspection, selected tinges of green, tan, and gray provide subtle effects. The hens, like most female ducks, wear camouflaging browns with slight differences in shades and patterns between the species.

Three of the species are quite robust and heavyset. In fact, at an average of 4.9 pounds for males, the common eider ranks as the leading heavyweight duck of the continent. The Steller's eider provides the exception to the eider size rule with its trim, mallard-like body.

In flight, the typical eider appears ponderous and sluggish, though it actually flies fairly fast. Flocks frequently travel single file, low to the water in long, undulating strings. This is especially true of the common eider, which has the colloquial name of "soldier duck." Its long troop-lines often travel so low they disappear between ocean swells. The common eider avoids flying over land when possible and in some places migrates hundreds of extra miles around peninsulas.

COMMON

The common eider is the species with which most people are familiar. Its breeding range extends from the Arctic all the way down to Maine. In winter, it may be routinely observed on the East Coast as far south as Long Island, and a few snowbirds even drift south to the Carolinas. A famous wintering spot lies offshore of Chatham, Massachusetts, where huge rafts of the birds gather. Unfortunately, Americans on the West Coast south of Alaska have little opportunity to see these striking sea ducks.

In the early days of exploration along the Canadian coast, colonies of hundreds of thousands of eiders were reported. Ships regularly visited these colonies for fresh eggs and stockpiles of meat. Not surprisingly, common eider populations suffered an extensive, long-term decline until legal pro-

Top: This photo shows the back and wing detail of a drake common eider. *Bottom:* This king eider hen is settled on her nest.

Above: The common eider hen has long been a source of the thick, soft down used in expensive quilts and jackets. *Facing page:* The back and breast of the common eider drake are white, while its belly is black. More subtle colors in the body feathers, and accent colors on the head and beak, add interest.

tection was provided in the early part of this century. The species has rebounded quite well thanks to strict enforcement of these laws.

KING

The king eider also enjoys a sizeable North American population, but is a less frequent visitor to the northeastern United States. It tends to be a more northerly bird whose haunts include the entire circumpolar region. Since the king eider does not nest in colonies, it has relatively little economic importance.

My first encounter with king eiders left a lasting, powerful impression about the harsh realities of an eider's life and nature's iron-fisted methods of population control. Nearly two decades ago, my father and I were photographing on Victoria Island in Canada's Northwest Territory, 200 miles north of the Arctic Circle. Of particular interest was the impressive variety of bird life that populates the brief but glorious summer. One day, we found two king eider nests, and then a snowy owl nest. The owl nest had four half-grown young; one eider nest had eggs that were hatching, and the other eider nest simply had eggs. We set up a blind on the owl nest. Then we went back and took some pictures of the eider sitting on eggs—she almost let us touch her as she sat rock still.

I felt a little sorry for this hen. Eiders do not eat for the 23 to 24 days they incubate, so she must have been quite hungry. Her nest was sheltered from the wind in a small depression and mosquitoes flourished in the calm air, copiously adorning her nostrils and other fleshy parts. In my opinion, the hen paid a heavy price for her wings—she couldn't swat at the mosquitoes to get even a small token of revenge against the tiny tormenters with a huge presence.

Just two days later, we saw the male snowy owl not far from the eider's nest and made only a passing comment about it. When we reached the owl nursery, a partially consumed carcass lay off to one side. Quickly putting two and two together, we checked the nest and, sure enough, the eider hen was gone and the eggs were getting cold. Adding to the tragedy was the fact that the eggs had started to pip. Perhaps the hen had stirred in response to this life beneath her, and the owl saw the movement—and wiped out the family.

Spectacled Eider Measurements

	Adult Male	Adult Female	Immature Male	Immature Female
Length	Average 20.8 in.	Average 19.6 in.		Average 19.8 in.
Wing	Average 9.80 in.	Average 9.61 in.	Average 9.49 in.	Average 9.41 in.
Weight	Average 3.25 lbs.	Average 3.22 lbs.		Average 2.75 lbs.

Common American Eider Measurements

	Adult Male	Adult Female
Length	22.5–26.8 in. Average 24.0	21.0–24.4 in. Average 22.8 in.
Wing	263–292 mm Average 277.8 mm	262–284 mm Average 270.6 mm
Weight	3.9–4.6 lbs. Average 4.38 lbs.	2.6–3.8 lbs. Average 3.38 lbs.

King Eider Measurements

	Adult Male	Adult Female
Length	21.7–25.0 in. Average 22.7 in.	18.5–22.5 in. Average 21.1 in.
Wing	Average 10.75	Average 10.37 in.
Weight*	Average 3.68 lbs.	Average 3.45 lbs.

* From Thompson and Person (1963)

Steller's Eider Measurements

	Adult Male	Adult Female
Length	17.5–18.5 in. Average 18.1 in.	17.1–18.1 in. Average 17.5 in.
Wing	8.23–8.54 in.	8.19–8.46 in.
Weight	1.87–2.12 lbs. Average 1.94 lbs.	1.87–2.00 lbs. Average 1.94 lbs.

Above: Who would have thought such contortionist's moves would be necessary for preening? *Facing page:* This common eider is in an excellent position for viewing his head and bill straight on.

The story continues. The very next day, the owls delivered half a dozen downy ducklings, one after another, to their nest. Each one was consumed by a nestling in one gulp. We located the "hatching" hen on her little brood pond, where she now swam all alone. The owls had systematically hunted down her entire brood.

The net reproductive result of these two eider females for the whole nesting season was the loss of one adult. This is perhaps not an unusual turn of events for eiders. Their reproductive success is low, yielding roughly a five to ten percent annual recruitment. On the other side of the ledger, adults tend to be long-lived, enjoying perhaps 20 years in the sun (or more likely, snow and ice). And of course, without some sort of population control, we would all soon be under a comforter of eider down, needed or not.

SPECTACLED AND STELLER'S

While both the king and common eider have sizeable North American populations, the spectacled eider is cur-

rently on the threatened list of the U.S. Fish and Wildlife Service. Its numbers have never been particularly large, a fact perhaps indicated by its limited nesting range. Most of the world's population occurs on a stretch of the western and northern coasts of Alaska. Small numbers of birds also breed along the Siberian coast. The spectacled eider winters somewhere in the Bering Sea, but other than that, "its winter range is not known" (Armstrong). The spectacled eider is slightly smaller than the king eider, which is slightly smaller than the common eider. Their lengths, in the same order, are 21, 22, and 24 inches.

The Steller's, as mentioned earlier, is cast from a different mold than its three brethren. Not only is it significantly shorter (at 18 inches), it also presents a more slender, agile appearance. Many observers liken its profile to a mallard's. Its weight is half that of the common eider.

The heart of the Steller's breeding range lies on the other side of the international dateline in Siberia. However,

Look at those black-rimmed glasses around this duck's white eye patches. It's easy to see where it gets the name "spectacled eider."

The common eider's breeding range extends from the Arctic to Maine, and in winter it may be found as far south as Long Island.

the primary wintering grounds for both American and Siberian birds extends from the eastern Aleutians to Kodiak Island. Wintering Steller's sometimes wander south to British Columbia.

FEEDING

Like all eiders, the Steller's dines primarily on animal matter. It favors soft-bodied crustaceans but also eats mollusks. The spectacled eider has similar tastes, while the king and common eiders rely more heavily on mussels, clams, barnacles, and related mollusks. Because of this "fishy" diet, eiders do not rank highly on the human table. The seafarers of yore, who harvested eiders in great numbers for their storage barrels, must have been hungry for meat indeed.

Eiders usually dive for food; they use their wings to "fly" through the water. The king eider is second only to the oldsquaw in diving depths and durations. King eiders have been captured in fishing nets at depths up to 150 feet.

Few ducks seem as rugged and stalwart in the face of the elements as our seafaring eiders. Though of stocky profile, they nevertheless present handsome images in their bold, black-and-white dress accented with sparing touches of color. Carvers may be torn between showing their talents with exquisite detail or capturing the essence of the eider in simpler, hardy shapes and strokes.

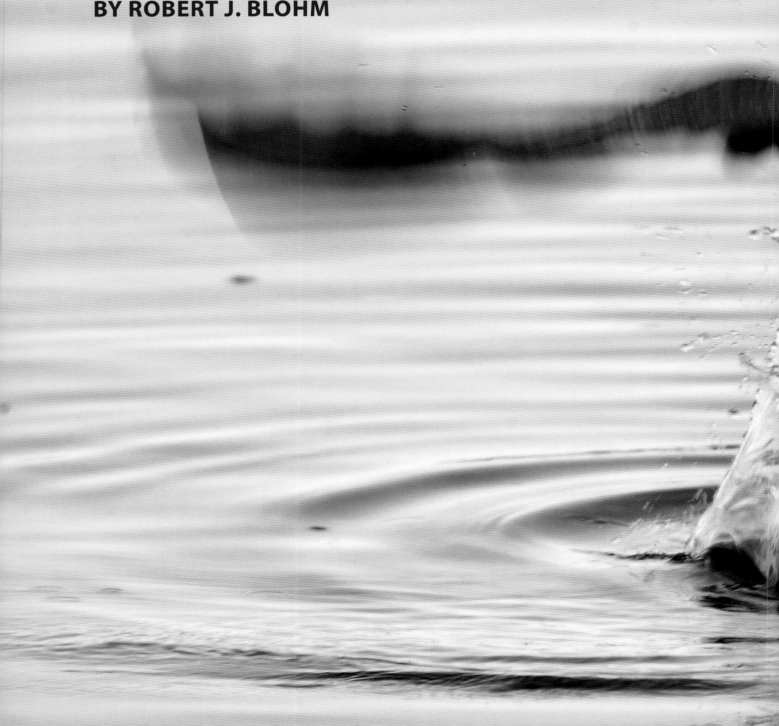

Gadwall
(*Anas strepera*)

BY ROBERT J. BLOHM

Opening pages: Something has startled this female gadwall into flight. Perhaps the photographer got too close for comfort. *Above:* The buff and brown coloration of the female provides good camouflage during the nesting season.

Although found over much of the northern hemisphere, the gadwall is one of the lesser known and least recognized ducks that frequent North American marshes and wetlands. It is classed as one of the dabbling, or puddle, ducks, a group that includes the mallard, pintail, blue-winged teal, and others known for their habit of feeding at the water's surface or tipping up to reach food.

At first glance, the gadwall appears to be rather bland-looking with little or no brilliant coloration to distinguish it from other species. This lack of distinction has no doubt caused some confusion in identification, resulting in such local names as gray mallard, prairie mallard, gray wigeon, wigeon, and the nondescript tag of gray duck, among others. A close inspection, however, particularly of the drake, reveals an intricate and beautiful pattern of design and coloration that is truly unique among North American waterfowl.

In the hand, the gadwall is smaller than the mallard but slightly larger than the American wigeon. Adult males in the fall normally weigh a little over two pounds, while adult hens average a quarter-pound or so less. Drakes in breeding plumage appear to be almost entirely gray with the exception of black hindquarters and a white belly and lower breast. Females resemble hen mallards in general ap-

pearance, but body feathers are more broadly edged with buff, while belly and lower breast feathers are white. In both sexes, bills are narrow, mostly black in the male and somewhat dusky with orange sides and some dark spotting in the female. In flight, the partially white speculum on the rear of the wing and sharply defined underparts distinguish this duck from others of similar size and shape.

THE GADWALL'S DISTRIBUTION

On this continent, the gadwall is known primarily as a duck of the prairies and during the breeding season is found in greatest numbers in the mixed grassland regions of southern Canada and the north central United States. High breeding densities are also associated with the aspen-parkland portions of Alberta, Saskatchewan, and Manitoba, with lower numbers observed in short-grass prairie areas of Canada and the United States and in intermountain marshes of some western states. Range extensions have occurred over the years, some with man's help, and now small breeding populations of gadwalls are reported in Alaska, the Great Lakes region, and along the East Coast, from New England south to the Carolinas.

Although the gadwall's abundance historically is a matter of conjecture, comparison of records and observations of gadwall numbers from the latter part of the last century with present-day information suggests marked changes in numbers and distribution of this species on its breeding range. The impact of man's settling of the prairie regions of the United States and Canada has undoubtedly been the biggest factor. In spite of man's alteration of the prairie landscape, the gadwall has been able to maintain a somewhat stable population level in recent years, but certainly not at its former abundance.

As one might expect, the wintering range of this species is quite widespread and diverse. Following the onset of fall migration, gadwalls wing their way to selected southern wintering grounds, stopping at traditional sites along the way. Although found in many states along the Atlantic and Pacific Coasts, by far the primary wintering area for this duck is the Gulf Coast. On the Gulf the gadwall gathers in greatest numbers during the winter months, particularly in Louisiana, which annually receives the major part of the migration. In the marshes and impoundments of the Gulf Coast, gadwalls spend most of their time feeding, selecting algae, wigeon grass, and other plants and seeds found commonly in these areas. Some birds stop along the coast only for a while and then continue on into Mexico and as far south as the Yucatan Peninsula and Central America.

Although not in the same category as mallards or canvasbacks in terms of delectable table fare, the gadwall is still sought by many hunters as a game and table duck and ranks high in the annual harvest in many parts of the country. Undoubtedly, however, some hunters confuse this duck with other species in flight, especially the hen mallard.

Not long after the close of the hunting season, gadwalls begin to leave the wintering grounds and make their way slowly back to northern latitudes. Some leave as early as February, but most begin the journey in March. During this trip north, they use all types of water areas that are ice-free and have available food as stopover points.

By April, few gadwalls remain in the south, while the early vanguard of arrivals begins to dot open waters in the northern Great Plains. In southern Canada, gadwalls appear in mid to late April and are soon followed by the majority of the migration. Generally speaking, however, this species is really considered to be a late arrival to the breeding grounds, having been preceded by such early migrants as mallards, pintails, canvasbacks, and others.

Alternating black and white lines on individual flank feathers give the male a zebra-like appearance at close range.

Gadwall Measurements				
	Adult Male	**Adult Female**	**Immature Male**	**Immature Female**
Length	19.5–22.5 in. Average 20.9 in.	18.2–20.2 in. Average 19.2 in.	18.5–21.7 in. Average 20.0 in.	18.0–19.5 in. Average 18.8 in.
Wing	10.7 in.	10.1 in.	10.5 in.	9.8 in.
Weight	1.6–2.3 lbs. Average 2.13 lbs.	1.4–2.3 lbs. Average 1.84 lbs.	1.3–2.3 lbs. Average 1.89 lbs.	1.1–2.1 lbs. Average 1.71 lbs.

Above: Here's a good view of the out-stretched wing of the male gadwall.
Left: The bill of the drake is usually slate gray or gray-black, and narrow. Breast feathers alternate black and white, appear crescent-shaped, and generally contain scattered flecking.

Most gadwalls are paired upon reaching northern breeding areas, having formed a pair bond already on southern wintering grounds or during the spring migration. As numbers increase, extra males appear, suggesting an imbalance in the sex ratio in favor of drakes. Early on, gadwalls often congregate in large groups, seemingly tolerant of other individuals nearby. This gregarious behavior provides little indication of the territorial conflicts that will soon follow as ducks disperse into smaller wetlands and prepare for the coming breeding activities.

Many of the early arrivals are transients, just passing through on their way to specific breeding areas elsewhere. Yet others will remain, having returned home to an area where they were hatched and raised in a previous year. Most biologists recognize the ability of waterfowl, especially females, to return to their natal area and thus take advantage of everything that familiar surroundings have to offer.

The gadwall hen is an excellent example of this behavior. Recent studies involving individually marked females have indicated extremely high return rates for this species, and in some cases, the same hen has been observed on a particular pond in two

Note the darker crown feathers, which sometimes give the head a slightly enlarged appearance. The intricate design and coloration of individual feathers on the breast, back, and flanks of the male dissolve into a generally gray appearance when observed from a distance.

The gadwall is one of ten species of North American dabbling ducks. Adults average about two pounds. White feathers at the rear of the wings are found in both sexes and differentiate this duck from other dabblers. Though highly conspicuous in flight, the white feathers may not always be visible when the duck is on the water.

or more years. In addition, these same marking studies have shown that some males, unpaired and not following a female to her own particular destination, will also go back to their natal area.

NESTING BEHAVIOR

Besides being a later traveler to northern breeding areas, the gadwall is also recognized for the long intervals between its first appearance in the spring and the onset of nesting. Normally a month or more may pass before egg-laying actually begins. Part of this time is spent on larger water areas in the company of other gadwalls or with species such as canvasbacks, redheads, or particularly American wigeon.

Soon, however, pairs disperse into smaller wetlands, selecting shallow marshes over temporary water bodies or deeper ponds. These wetlands, often alkaline, are teeming with small animal foods that appear to be essential in the diet of breeding ducks in the spring. In the pothole country of the northern United States and southern Canada, gadwalls prefer alkaline wetlands more than most other duck species.

At this time, pairs establish "activity centers" that include one or more preferred feeding and loafing sites, and spend most of the day here. This pre-nesting period signals the beginning of intense activity on the marsh as tolerance

levels between pairs disappear and conflicts over territory and space become commonplace.

The basis for this intolerance is relatively straightforward. Preferred sites that provide all of the requisites of the reproductive cycle—places to feed, loaf, and bathe near favorite nesting covers—are sometimes at a premium. For those that already occupy these areas, there are always other pairs around seeking to displace the original owners.

A predictable sequence of events takes place when a pair lands on a currently occupied pond. The resident drake chases the visitors away, pursuing them for some distance as he focuses his attack on the intruding female. His own mate remains on the pond. If one is fortunate enough to witness one of these three-bird flights in the spring, you notice not only the wild acrobatics of the pursuit flight but also the noise of the chase.

The air is filled with the rapid series of nasal-pitched calls of the drake and the hen's more harsh quacking. In addition, you may hear the sound of actual wing and body contact as the two drakes collide while jockeying for position behind the fleeing female. The length of the flight varies but when it is over, the resident drake returns to his pond and his mate.

As nesting nears, this territorial behavior increases in frequency, intensity, and duration, with resident drakes

Top: For nesting, pairs select shallow marshes over temporary water bodies or deeper ponds. These wetlands are teeming with small animal foods that appear to be essential in the diet of breeding ducks in the spring. *Bottom:* There must be something yummy down there. Bottoms up!

even initiating chase flights at approaching pairs flying nearby. Many theories have been proposed regarding the function of chasing behavior in ducks. One important and obvious advantage of the aggressive behavior of the gadwall male in particular is to protect the food supply of selected areas and ensure undisturbed feeding time for his mate as she prepares for the nesting cycle.

Just prior to egg-laying, a resident pair will search together for a suitable nesting site, flying low over prospective cover before landing. Then, on the ground, the actual location is chosen by the female and before long, she scrapes one or more potential nest bowls. Gadwall hens prefer well-drained upland areas not far from water that provide dense cover, such as impoundment dikes, unhayed fields, and old-growth areas.

Because they are late nesters, gadwalls can take advantage of substantial new growth as well as any residual cover from the previous season, all providing a well-concealed site in the thick matrix of vegetation. Some of these areas are used year after year. From observations of marked ducks, biologists have found female gadwalls returning to within a few feet of a previous year's successful nest site, attesting to the suitability of a particular cover and the homing ability of individual ducks.

INCUBATION

Generally gadwall females lay one egg a day early in the morning while the drake remains nearby at the activity center waiting for her return. The nest

bowl changes in appearance daily during laying as the hen gradually adds vegetative material, down, and body feathers to the bowl, providing a camouflaged, cushioned compartment for her eggs. As the number of eggs increases, she spends more time at the nest and by the end of laying, she has effectively established her incubation rhythm.

The size of a completed clutch depends upon a number of factors, including date of laying and age of the hen. Studies have indicated that adult gadwall hens (two years or older) usually nest earlier and lay larger clutches than yearling females. Although initial clutches may range in number from eight to 13 eggs, nests of adult hens usually contain about ten eggs per

Unlike geese and swans, the pair bond in most ducks is not permanent but rather dissolves during the breeding season. In the gadwall, most pair bonds are severed by mid-incubation. This breakup occurs gradually as the drake spends more and more time away from the activity center and begins to seek the company of other males. Territorial flights decline and, when associated with other males, formerly paired drakes may focus their attention on other hens.

It is not uncommon at this time to see groups of drakes engaged in long, harrying flights across the marsh in pursuit of an unfortunate female. These post-breeding groups soon become large congregations gathering on favored areas that offer security during the flightless period of the molt. Here, they begin the critical regrowth of body and wing feathers, and their presence on these areas signals the advancing of the breeding season.

As the days pass in incubation, females spend most of their recess time away from the nest feeding to help keep up with the rigors of this part of the nesting cycle. Then just prior to hatch, hens become more attentive than ever to the nest, with little time off, even for feeding. Within a day or two, her young will appear.

In addition to what might be termed "normal" nesting behavior, the gadwall has developed a rather unique reproductive strategy not shared by many other waterfowl. That behavior is the tendency of females to gather together for what is best described as social nesting. Generally most female ducks will space their nests widely throughout preferred habitats. The

nest, while nests of yearlings average about nine eggs.

Gadwalls are also considered to be persistent re-nesters. In the event that the initial nest is destroyed by predators or lost due to other factors, a hen may begin again, one or more times, in an attempt to raise a brood of young. Clutch sizes of such re-nesting efforts are generally smaller than the initial attempt.

The incubation period for the gadwall averages about 24–26 days. During this period, the hen alternates time between the nest and feeding and loafing areas. Upon leaving the nest site, she carefully hides the eggs beneath a covering of vegetation, feathers, and down, making them nearly invisible to the unsuspecting eye. Whether or not her mate will be waiting for her when she returns from her "recess" period varies.

The gadwall's silhouette is cleanly outlined against the morning sunrise sky.

gadwall does this as well. If conditions are right, however, some ducks—the gadwall in particular—will choose to nest in extremely high densities.

In recent years, investigators have studied this extraordinary behavior of gadwalls and other species on islands in the northern United States and southern Canada. Their findings are rather spectacular. In the thick vegetation that characterizes many of these places, including formidable plants such as stinging nettle, workers have found large numbers of hens nesting in a relatively small area, unusually large clutches, and at times, extremely high nesting success.

The number of eggs in these nests has sometimes reached as many as 24 and indicates that more than one hen has contributed to the nest. These large clutches are not surprising in light of the nesting density and an individual hen's chances for error in returning to the correct bowl day after day.

Whether a hen gadwall nests alone in a grassy field or with many others on an island, the ultimate goal is the same: successful reproduction. Because of the length of time required for laying and incubating a clutch, many hazards can disrupt the whole process, resulting in nest destruction and, in some cases, death of the hen. The gadwall's late nesting tendency and preference for dense cover has its advantages. Combined with the varied strat-egy for nesting, the probability for success in producing a brood is relatively good, perhaps more so than for some other species.

During the seven to eight weeks required to fledge, ducklings and hen are observed spending a great deal of time feeding, mostly on aquatic invertebrates at first, and then changing over to a more herbivorous diet. For the young, food energy is used for general growth and development of their first plumage.

For the hen, feeding now provides nutrients and energy necessary for the annual molt of wing and body feathers and recovery from the draining activities of incubation. Depending on the timing of her nesting efforts, she may remain with her young for a long period, or desert them early when a late hatch allows her little time to replace her feathers in preparation for the flight south.

By the end of summer, the breeding season for gadwalls draws to a close. Drakes and hens begin to show signs that signal the coming of fall. Old ducks appear, renewed in plumage from the recent molt and able to fly once more, while young birds are preparing to take to the wing for the first time. It is a period of gathering into large flocks and, as early as the first part of September in southern Canada, these flocks begin to wing southward to wintering grounds. For this unique and interesting species, another cycle has been completed and a new one is just beginning.

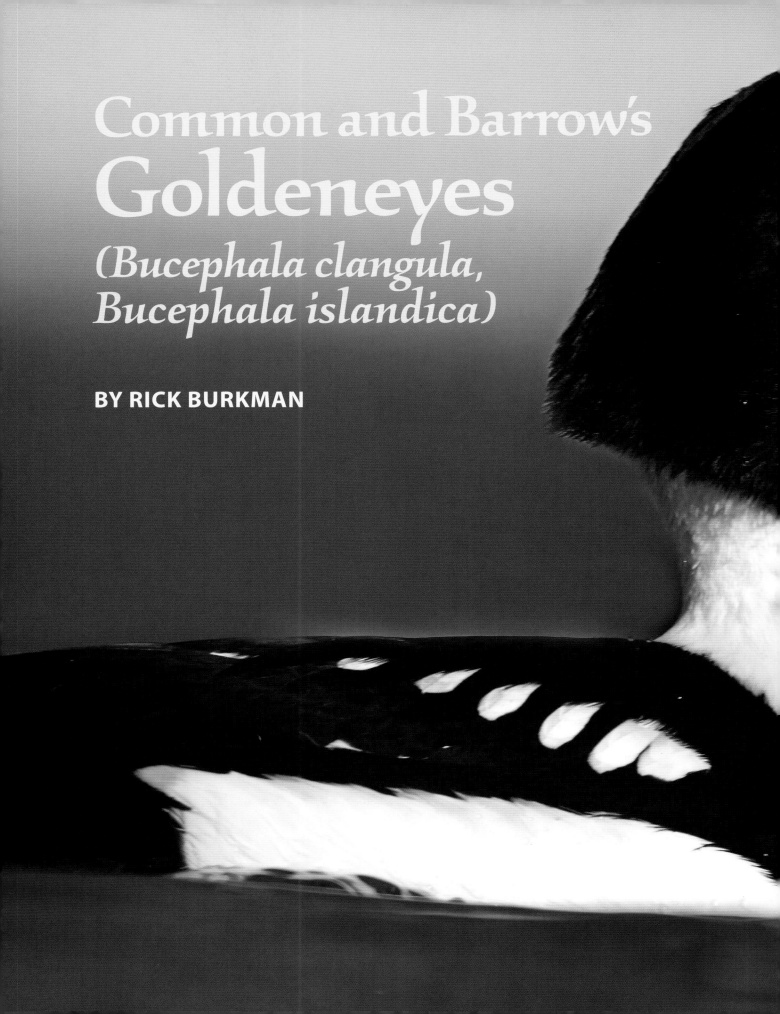

Common and Barrow's Goldeneyes

(Bucephala clangula, Bucephala islandica)

BY RICK BURKMAN

Opening pages: The Barrow's goldeneye's head and bill protrude forward more than those of the common goldeneye, which has a more gently sloping silhouette. *Above:* Goldeneye ducklings are easy to identify by their white cheek patches. Though the hens carefully watch over their young as they make the trek from tree nest to water, the family bond dissolves by six weeks of age.

People don't often think of goldeneyes as seasonal indicators, as they do with the first robin of spring or the autumnal skeins of wild geese veeing south for the winter. But savvy nature watchers know that big changes are about to occur when the first goldeneyes show up to feed in the cold autumn lakes. Likewise, when the winter ice breaks and the goldeneyes dance as they swim, the first yellow days of spring are not far behind. The life-cycle of these cold-hardy ducks makes a grand circuit that keeps them in tune with the season's cycles.

North America has two resident goldeneye species that cross the continent in their annual journeys. The common goldeneye travels from the northern boreal forests to the Atlantic coast and back each year. Its scientific name, *Bucephala clangula*, literally means "big head, whistle wings," a reference to its rounded head and the way its wings whistle in flight. The Barrow's goldeneye (*Bucephala islandica*, which translates as "big head Icelandic" because it was first discovered in Iceland) prefers the montane forests of northwestern North America and it winters in the Pacific coastal areas. Barrow's goldeneyes and common goldeneyes are sim-

ilar in appearance, but can be distinguished by head shape. The common goldeneye has a sloped head and bill silhouette, whereas the Barrow's goldeneye head protrudes forward, giving the bird a look reminiscent of a cartoon alien.

Both goldeneye species end the winter and start the spring filled with energy and vigor. Unpaired males find unattached females and court them to distraction. Males point their bills upward and outward then lift and move their heads in backward arcs that end with the backs of their heads sitting atop their rumps. Once in this odd position the male gives a backward kick with his feet shooting a small spray of water behind him as an added display. Females may join in this strange dance by pointing their bills forward and stretching their necks, but they do not hyperextend their necks backward like the males.

NESTING

Eventually, the birds stop displaying and begin the all-important job of starting a family.

Goldeneyes are northern breeders and make their nesting homes in the boreal forests of the subarctic,

where summers are short and autumn may be non-existent. Because time is short the goldeneyes do not waste it building a pretty nest. Instead, they quickly find an abandoned tree cavity, preferably with an old squirrel or bird nest already in place (or at least some sawdust and wood chips). Once she finds a suitable cavity the hen immediately begins nesting. She adds a few feathers from her own body, either plucking them during preening or as she exposes her brood spot.

Egg laying begins as soon as the nest cavity is chosen. The hen lays one olive-colored egg every other day until she has a clutch of 8 to 10. She incubates the eggs for about 30 days before they begin hatching. By then the male has departed, abandoning

Above right: The drake common goldeneye has a greenish-black head and a bright oval white patch on the side of its face at the base of its bill. *Right:* The sides, breast, belly, and secondaries are bright white, and the back, wings, and tail are black.

Common Goldeneye Measurements*

	Culmen	Wing Length	Tarsus	Length	Weight
Male	30–44 mm	215–247 mm	35–47 mm	17.9–20.2 in. Average 17.0 in.	2.0–3.2 lbs. Average 2.37 lbs.
Female	28–37 mm	188–229 mm	32–49 mm	15.7–19.7 in. Average 17.0 in.	1.6–2.8 lbs. Average 1.74 lbs.

* From Eadie, et. al., and Bellrose

Barrow's Goldeneye Measurements*

	Culmen	Wing Length	Tarsus	Length	Weight
Male	31–36 mm	228–248 mm	40–43 mm	18.6–19.9 in. Average 19.2 in.	1.5–2.5 lbs. Average 2.13 lbs.**
Female	28–34 mm	205–230 mm	37–40 mm	16.2–17.7 in. Average 17.0 in.	1.1–1.8 lbs. Average 1.31 lbs.

* From Eadie, et. al., and Bellrose
** These weights are of flightless birds captured at Ohtig Lake, Alaska (Yocum 1970).

The common goldeneye coming . . . and going. Note the shape of the head and the golden yellow eyes.

the hen after the first week or two of incubation to join other males on open-water lakes for a pre-migration molt. (The hens choose their own molting lakes and will join together at a later time.)

Many waterfowl have the curious habit of sneaking over to a neighbor's nest when she is away and quickly depositing an egg there so its hatchling will grow with the owner's brood. Actually, sneaking in may be a bit misleading. A goldeneye will fly into a nest hole at full speed, stalling at the last moment and pivoting into the cavity like a gymnast as its feet hit the bottom of the nest opening.

Goldeneyes are not choosy where they dump eggs. They pick the nests of hooded mergansers, smews (a kind of Asiatic merganser), and wood ducks. Turnabout is fair play in the duck world and it is equally likely that those ducks will dump their eggs in goldeneye nests. A hen will diligently incubate all of the eggs she finds in her nest, but she may abandon her efforts if the egg count reaches 20 or more.

When incubation is complete the new ducklings kick free from their shells, their soft dark downy feathers already in place. Although it will take a couple of hours for their down to dry the ducklings quickly gain control over their tiny feet and stubby wings. Their dark, bright eyes are alert and contrast sharply with their large white cheek patch.

After waiting a day for all of the eggs to hatch and for the ducklings to develop some body strength, the hen decides it is time for the young to venture into the world. She leaves the nest, flapping back and forth between the ground and the cavity opening as she coaxes the nestlings out of their tall tree home. Eventually one becomes brave enough to plunge into space in a vain attempt to fly. The little bird tumbles to the ground instead, twisting through the air until it hits the forest floor, its light weight saving it from harm. Once the first duckling makes the jump the others tumble out of the hole in rapid succession. When all of the young have left the nest the hen marches the brood to a rearing lake, sometimes a trek of several miles, where they will feed on the multitude of invertebrates that thrive in the waters of a boreal summer forest.

YOUNG DUCKS

Mother goldeneyes do not fit our expectations of responsible parents. Young goldeneye families will mix with other ducklings on the rearing lake and, in the mix up, several may end up following a new mother as part of a large crèche of ducklings comprised of birds from many broods.

This occurs because the child-parent bond is not strong in goldeneyes. Some mothers abandon their young as early as one week after hatching, but most wait until the birds are about five or six weeks old. Even the mothers who stick around that long still leave their family two weeks before the young birds can fly. No matter—young goldeneyes are quite independent and capable of surviving on their own, even at this young age.

After the females abandon their parenting duties they form a molting flock, resting on a roosting lake for a few weeks as they replace feathers and fatten up on scuds, mollusks, and insect larvae. Seasons are changing and these birds want to be ready to fly when the weather cools.

This photo of the common goldeneye is the perfect starting place for a high-head duck decoy.

This male is fanning his wings, perhaps trying to impress a potential mate. Goldeneyes make elaborate breeding displays, pointing their bills upward and outward and arcing their backs until their heads sit atop their rumps, all the while kicking water spray.

Young birds begin migrating south after their first feathers fill in, which happens about the same time their molting mothers are ready to migrate. Now the youngsters resemble their mothers. They have a brown or chestnut head, dark bill with a yellow tip (although Western populations of Barrow's goldeneye females have all-yellow bills), and a gray body with white wing markings. Adult males, on the other hand, are dapper and striking, a combination of crisp white areas and barring, along with a white patch located below and in front of the eye and behind the bill. The patch is oval in the common goldeneye and crescent-shaped in the Barrow's. Both males and females have a dark iris centered in a bright yellow eye that gives them their common name.

The goldeneyes are relatively common migrants. They have little tolerance for changes in water quality so their presence should make us feel good about the conservation efforts on our waterways. But when the goldeneyes show up, prepare yourself for seasonal change.

REFERENCES

Eadie, John M., Jean-Pierre L. Savard and Mark L. Mallory. 2000. Barrow's Goldeneye (Bucephala islandica), The Birds of North America Online (A. Poole, Ed.). Ithaca: Cornell Lab of Ornithology; Retrieved from the Birds of North America Online: http://bna.birds.cornell.edu/bna/species/548doi:10.2173/bna.548

Eadie, J. M., M. L. Mallory and H. G. Lumsden. 1995. Common Goldeneye (Bucephala clangula), The Birds of North America Online (A. Poole, Ed.). Ithaca: Cornell Lab of Ornithology; Retrieved from the Birds of North America Online: http://bna.birds.cornell.edu/bna/species/170doi:10.2173/bna.170

Top: The female Barrow's goldeneye has a chocolate brown head; slate gray back, wings, and tail; white flanks, belly, and breast; pale yellow to white eyes; and a short, mostly yellow, triangular bill. *Bottom:* Though adult male common goldeneye eyes are bright yellow, they start out gray-brown, and then turn purple-blue, then blue, then green-blue as they age. By five months of age they have become a clear pale green-yellow.

Green-winged Teal
(Anas crecca)

BY JEROME A. JACKSON

Opening pages: The green of the wing of the green-winged teal is often hidden, but it can clearly be seen on the flying hen in this photo. *Above:* It seems that the green-winged teal could have been just as aptly named "green-headed" due to the bright green eye stripe the male displays.

"Yeow!" With a splash I ended up sitting in five inches of water staring skyward through the weeds at a rapidly departing duck. I'm sure I screamed, though there was probably not a soul within two miles to hear me. One minute I was easing as quietly as possible along the flooded edge of a grassy field, the next I was sitting in the water. The muddy field was uneven and slick. When the birds exploded from almost beneath my feet, it was all I could do to land sitting!

It was a cold January day in 1987, and I was searching a backwater swamp of the Pascagoula River in coastal Mississippi for evidence of perhaps the rarest bird in the world: the ivory-billed woodpecker. I had been scanning some ancient oaks and sweetgums ahead and to my right and ignoring things close at hand when the pair of green-winged teal leapt into the air with a whistled scream and a hoarse croak.

Although I had seen numerous wood ducks and hooded mergansers earlier in the day, I wasn't at all thinking "duck." But green-winged teal are pretty tame birds, sometimes allowing a close approach. They stick to shallow water and grassy areas, where they feed on seeds and are capable of leaping straight up and winging away if need be. Such behavior has even entered our language in the old hunter's term for a group of green-wings: a "spring" of teal. Green-winged teal are among the fastest and most agile of ducks, often exceeding 40 miles per hour as they twist and turn in tight flocks in the manner of shorebirds. Although 50 miles per hour is probably stretching it, one estimate of maximum flight speed for the green-winged teal was 160 miles per hour, achieved perhaps with a very hefty tail wind!

My delayed recognition of the species was reinforced as the sprites circled and flew back over my head toward the river, as if checking to see what had startled them. That's just like green-wings, too. Hunters of the nineteenth century found they could sometimes slap a paddle against the side of their boat and these teal would come back to investigate. A flock thus disturbed might return more than once, making them very vulnerable to the skilled market hunter.

The green-wing is our smallest puddle duck, barely 15 inches long from bill to tail when stretched out. Just a mere handful of a duck, it's about the size of a hefty pigeon. Males are only slightly larger than females in most dimensions, but much brighter in plumage. The word "teal" may have come from the Old English *tele*, which meant "small." The scientific name for the green-wing—*Anas crecca*—includes the genus *Anas*, to which many of our ducks belong, and the species name *crecca*, which may be mimetic of the common whistled call of the male.

The whistled calls of males are significantly different from and more complex than the typical female's quack. The whistled *creek-et* call that males often give in winter and spring carries a great distance, sometimes announcing this teal's presence before it is seen. It's the male that seems more engaged in social banter, while the female attends to getting into condition for migration and the domestic duties of nest building, incubation, and care of the young.

The belly of the male green-wing is white, shading up to buff on the breast and then a slight ring of gray on the neck. The breast appears tawny buff to pinkish cinnamon, and is sparingly spotted with black.

Green-winged Teal Measurements				
	Adult Male	**Adult Female**	**Immature Male**	**Immature Female**
Length	13.7–15.5 in. Average 14.7 in.	13.0–14.5 in. Average 13.9 in.	12.1–15.2 in. Average 13.8 in.	12.1–14.0 in. Average 13.4 in.
Wing	7.3 in.	7.0 in.	7.2 in.	6.9 in.
Weight	0.5–1.1 lbs. Average 0.71 lb.	0.4–1.1 lbs. Average 0.68 lb.	0.3–1.1 lbs. Average 0.72 lb.	0.3–0.9 lb. Average 0.64 lb.

Top: The green-winged teal prefers shallow ponds with lots of emergent vegetation. Along the coast, it prefers mudflats, tidal creeks, and marshes to more open water.
Bottom: This hen green-wing gives us a great look at her foot and the underside of her bill as she scratches her neck.

HABITAT AND MIGRATION

American green-winged teal nest from Alaska across much of Canada and the western United States and at scattered localities in the north-central and northeastern United States south to coastal Maryland. Breeding Bird Surveys suggest the greatest numbers of green-winged teal nest in central Alberta and Saskatchewan, west-central British Columbia, southern Manitoba, North Dakota, and in the intermountain western United States. They winter where there are ice-free waters through most of the United States and parts of southern Canada. From October to March, a few can be found enjoying shallow freshwater ponds and marshes of the Bahamas and West Indies. A few even show up in Central America and northern South America.

The American and Eurasian greenwings are, for the moment, considered the same species by the American Ornithologists' Union, but separation of the two is one of those points of contention that seems to flow back and forth with each new bit of knowledge of the birds. The Eurasian race is sometimes found in North America, and its Yankee relative reciprocates with visits to Europe. The two races interbreed, but can be told apart readily by the vertical white line, or crescent, that extends down from near the bend of the folded wing of males of the American race and the horizontal white line that extends above the wing on each side of males of the Eurasian race. Females of the two races are generally indistinguishable.

There are two peaks in the fall migration of green-winged teal: middle to late August and November. Greenwings frequently associate with bluewinged teal during migration, particularly early in the season, often leaving nesting areas in mid-August. Males may leave the nesting area for better feeding and a warmer climate, but don't go far before they stop at a

The under-tail area is whitish-buff colored, and the rump is black. The sides of the duck are finely vermiculated black and white.

The male deserts the female during the early stages of egg incubation and leaves her to raise her brood alone. Ducklings follow their mother from the time they are a day old.

safe haven to undergo their fall molt. Late migrants tend to arrive in the southern United States in pure green-wing flocks in November. Timing of arrival varies from year to year—earlier in bad winters, later in mild winters. The green-winged teal is one of the last ducks to abandon good feeding in more northern areas, waiting until ponds and marshes are freezing over. Clearly this is a bird that is benefiting from warmer winters.

The timing of migration of green-winged teal also varies with age, sex, and nesting success. Older males tend to lead the way southward in fall. Those that are successful with early nests leave first, followed by later nesting males and females that didn't raise a brood. Females with broods are generally the last to leave for the winter.

This is a classic puddle duck—one that nests in freshwater marshes, lakes, and ponds that are surrounded by grasses and weeds. Courtship also takes place in such

marshes and shallows and is very intense, beginning in mid-winter. Wintering flocks of green-wings can number in the hundreds, providing abundant opportunities for social interaction and courtship. Green-wings are monogamous, but two dozen or more males may besiege a single female or group of females. Most courtship takes place in the water and includes male displays with such descriptive and whimsical sounding names as the "burp" (head raised, loud whistle given), the "grunt-whistle" (one or two head shakes followed by an arching of the neck and back while pointing the bill downward and flicking it toward the female), and the "down-up" (tail and back part of the body are raised and lowered as the bird gives short whistles).

BREEDING AND FEEDING

Male green-winged teal are intensely combative in spring, challenging each new arrival. Although most green-wings are paired by the time they migrate north in spring, courtship continues en route and some courtship displays and chases can be seen on the nesting grounds. Most nests are close to water in grasses. The female builds the nest and typically lays an egg a day to complete a clutch of five to sixteen creamy white eggs. Once she begins incubating, the male leaves her and may join with other males to begin his southward migration.

Incubation lasts 21 to 23 days. At hatching, the hen leads her brood to nearby water, where they feed extensively on small invertebrates and succulent plants. The ducklings grow rapidly, and may be capable of flight within about five weeks.

Green-wings feed extensively on mud flats, but they are also dabblers—ducks that tip up to grope around beneath the surface for delectables such as seeds of nutgrasses, millet, bulrushes, and other pond weeds. They also eat duckweed, leaves of watercress, and other aquatic plants, as well as insect larvae and a host of other small creatures.

When it's feeding time and "bottoms up" for teal, each black and buff colored bottom tends to blend in with clumps of dried weeds. Even on migration and in winter, a green-wing seeks out shallow water with emergent weeds for feeding and shelter, though it sometimes sleeps bobbing in deeper, more open water with its head tucked into its scapular feathers. As the green-wing sits on the water, it rides high, clearly showing the gray sides, the dark tail with its buff triangle surrounded by black on each side and the speckled breast. At midday, green-winged teal are usually loafing; at dusk they tend to become quite active.

PLUMAGE

As Audubon pointed out in the early 1800s, the name "green-winged" is not a particularly enlightening choice

Top: The rich chestnut brown of the male's slightly crested head is flashily adorned with a rich, silky, iridescent green teardrop extending from just in front of each eye to the nape. *Bottom:* The chin of the male green-wing is dark gray-brown to black. Most of the upper contour feathers are gray to creamy white with fine vermiculations of black.

for a common name since this teal doesn't have any more green on its wing than some other species. The green that is present on the wing is a bright iridescent green limited to only a few inner secondaries. The first few secondaries are a velvet black, and so are a few inward from the iridescent green. The secondaries are bordered by a margin of rufous secondary coverts. The outer black secondaries and first two or three green ones are tipped with white.

While the green wings of this duck are usually rather inconspicuous, the rich chestnut brown of the male's slightly crested head is flashily adorned with a rich, silky, iridescent green teardrop extending from just in front of each eye to the nape like the halo and tail of a comet. The tails of the teardrops meet at the nape in a slight mane. The feathers between the eye and the front edge of the green face mask are rich maroon. In the American green-winged teal, this teardrop of green is edged below with tawny black and is ringed with a fine, sometimes broken, pinstripe of buff to yellow. An additional, often broken, light line borders the

upper bill and extends back toward the upper front edge of the green mask. In the Eurasian green-winged teal, the pinstriping is much more continuous and conspicuous.

The chin of male green-wings is dark gray-brown to black. Most of the upper contour feathers are gray to creamy white with fine vermiculations of black. There is a black band along the outer vane of most scapular feathers, and these join to give the appearance of a longitudinal bar above the folded wing.

The male green-wing's belly is white, shading to a vertically vermiculated gray on the sides and buff pink on the breast. The gray of the sides blends into the buff breast. At the neck, a slight ring of gray often separates the chestnut of the head and neck from the buff of the breast. The breast appears as a rich tawny buff to almost pinkish cinnamon, sparingly spotted with black. The spots vary from round to almost heart-shaped, are centered on the feather shaft, and are located just back from the lighter feather tip so that they become more conspicuous as the lighter tip

The teardrop of green on the drake's face is edged below with tawny black and ringed with a fine pinstripe of buff to yellow. An additional, often broken, light line borders the upper bill and extends back toward the upper front edge of the green mask.

wears. Breast spots I measured were nearly round and ranged in diameter from two to three millimeters. From the vent to the tail is black, but is bordered on each side by a triangle of light buff to cream-colored feathers. Tail feathers are pointed and dark gray to almost black. The two central tail feathers are more pointed than the others and extend slightly beyond the others.

When one thinks "duck," the first characteristic that comes to mind is often the broad duck bill epitomized by farmyard mallards and Daffy, Donald, and Daisy of the cartoon world. Forget that with the green-wing. The green-wing's leathery bill is black in the male. In the female breeding plumage, it is greenish-gray with dark spots on the side. The bill of both sexes is probably narrower than the average carver's little finger—it is just about half an inch wide and tapers very little so that the edges of the bill seem to remain parallel. The upper bill is slightly enlarged at the tip with a conspicuous hard nail that protects the rest of the bill as the duck grovels around in mud and sand for its food. The nail extends slightly downward at the tip, giving the bill somewhat of a hooked appearance. Legs and feet of the green-wing are gray to gray-flesh colored, with the webs darker gray to nearly black. The claw on each toe is black and about seven millimeters long. A green-wing's eyes are a rich dark brown.

Green-wings have long been considered among the tastiest of ducks, and were common in southern markets during fall and winter. Some hunters figured these little birds out and were able to shoot dozens in a single day. Though bigger ducks were favored because of their size, green-winged teal populations declined during the late 1800s and early 1900s.

The drake looks like he's about to go after a meal, while the hen is relaxing during an afternoon siesta.

With the introduction of bag limits and hunting seasons, green-wings quickly rebounded and their populations have held fairly steady. Early declines seem to have been purely a function of over-hunting.

The reason for such a success story with green-winged teal is that this is not a duck that is heavily dependent on the prairie pothole habitats of the northern United States and southern Canada, nor is it a bird dependent on cavities in the old trees of bottomland hardwood forests, as wood ducks are. Although some green-winged teal nest in the eastern United States, most green-wing breeding populations nest in parts of Canada and the western United States that have thus far been little affected by the habitat changes that have wrought havoc on populations of other species.

Some loss of breeding, wintering and stopover habitats as well as pollution from intensive agriculture and mining activities present continuing threats for green-winged teal, but annual censuses are reassuring. Thanks to a growing network of state, federal, and private wetland refuges and continued purchase and management of wetlands by Ducks Unlimited and other conservation groups, we can continue to enjoy springs of teal as these birds make their way on their annual treks across America.

Long-tailed Duck
(Clangula hyemalis)

BY SHERYL DE VORE

In fall, when the cold winds fore-shadowing winter return to the northern United States and southern Canada, so, too, returns the long-tailed duck (formerly known as the oldsquaw). This hardy duck breeds farther north than any other duck, and its Latin name, *Clangula hyemalis*, reflects that fact. *Hyemalis* means "of or related to winter." Having left its Arctic breeding grounds, the oldsquaw winters on the frigid waters of the Great Lakes and the coasts where it dives perhaps deeper than any other duck to feed on crustaceans, mollusks, other small animals, and occasionally plant life of the sea.

The long-tailed duck tumbles in the air as if riding a fast and well-curved roller coaster. One of the fastest of ducks, it often flies close to the water, bending and turning to display a rich, dark breast and calling a

Opening pages: The long-tailed duck is the trimmest of the sea ducks. Its body is tapered much more than that of the eider or scoter. *Top:* When displaying, the male may erect his tail and stiffen his neck. He will then lower his head, holding his bill outward and upward as he calls to the female. *Bottom:* The female's bill is dark in winter, and she has more white on her cheeks than she does in summer and more dark coloration on her head than the male.

nasal, *Ow. Ow. Owdoolette*—a call which is said to have reminded Indian braves of the sound of an old squaw, hence, the name oldsquaw. Outside of North America the species was known as the long-tailed duck and that is now its name on this continent, too, in part because Native Americans came to consider the word "squaw" as offensive. In announcing the change in 2000 the American Ornithologists' Union Committee on Classification and Nomenclature said, "The Committee declines to consider political correctness alone in changing long-standing English names of birds but is willing in this instance to adopt an alternative name that is in use in much of the world."

PLUMAGE PATTERNS

Apart from its uniqueness as the hardiest and fastest of ducks, the long-tailed duck also possesses one of the most unusual plumage patterns of ducks, presenting a challenge to a carver's creativity.

Like most other ducks, the long-tailed duck's plumage differs from male to female. However, its summer and winter plumages are more distinct than any other duck.

In breeding plumage, during the summer months, the male's head sports a rich black-brown color with white space around the eye. "The

The long-tailed duck's head is a smooth oval shape. A pinkish-orange V is apparent on his dark bill.

Long-tailed Duck Measurements				
	Adult Male	**Adult Female**	**Immature Male**	**Immature Female**
Length	19.0–22.6 in. Average 20.8 in.	14.8–17.2 in. Average 15.6 in.		
Wing	8.7 in.	8.3 in.	8.2 in.	7.8 in.
Weight	2.00–2.22 lbs.	1.65–1.82 lbs.	1.88–2.07 lbs.	1.60–1.81 lbs.

A circle of dark brown and black on the back of his neck sets off the drake's whitish-gray head and throat.

Long-tailed ducks feed at depths of 10 meters or more. They dive deeper than any other duck for food, and have been caught in fishermen's nets set as deep as 35 meters.

feathers of the upper back and scapulars are broadly edged with brown and the rest of the head, neck, breast, back, and wings are a deep, rich, seal brown," writes Arthur Cleveland Bent in *Life Histories of North American Wild Fowl*. This deep brown makes a striking contrast with the white belly.

In August, the male long-tailed duck begins to assume his winter plumage and by the time he has reached his wintering grounds, he dons a great deal more white—a white that appears as pristine as newly fallen snow. A circle of dark brown and black beneath his eyes sets off his pure white head and neck. White primary feathers fold over dark brown secondary feathers.

Observers can identify a male in all plumages by its long tail. The long, slender tail is dark year-round and can measure up to 13 centimeters in length. In most plumages, the bill of the male is black at the tip and close to its head with orange in between. In all seasons, the duck can be identified by its compact, rounded head, short neck, small bill, all dark wings, and dark breast.

The female, of course, appears drabber and does not have a long tail. Her bill is dark in winter, but bears a washed-out gray color with soft splashes of cream in summer. In winter, the female dons considerable amounts of brown on her body with more white on her cheeks than in summer and more dark coloration on her head than the male.

During breeding time, the female long-tailed duck wears more subdued colors, which help her blend in with her surroundings when nesting. Her body is white and there is a touch of white around her eye and neck.

COURTSHIP AND NESTING

The male still wears his striking winter plumage when he begins to court the female. Long-tailed ducks begin forming pair bonds as early as January and as spring nears, large groups of males crowd around chosen females calling their *ow, ow, owdoolettes* and vying for attention.

The male may erect his tail, stiffen his neck and then lower his head, holding his bill outward and upward as he

calls to the female. Sometimes he will hold his head out along the water and the female will repeat his actions, uttering her own responding notes. The male may also throw his head back, pointing to the sky and calling.

In spring, between March 15 and April 15, hundreds of long-tailed ducks will stop by at the Chesapeake Bay and along other migratory routes on their way back to the Arctic. When they reach the Arctic, they will remain in large flocks offshore, feeding and waiting for the thaw that will open up the tundra pools and lakes where they will stay all summer.

The duck's breeding range extends from Alaska to the Canadian archipelago and up along the Arctic coast. In the southern hemisphere, the range includes the Antarctic coastline.

The female makes her nest in grasses near freshwater ponds or among rocks farther away from water, adding a lining of grass to a hollow in the ground. She lays five to seven smooth, oval, olive-buff eggs and covers them with her dull brown down for camouflage. She incubates alone while the male hovers nearby for a period of time before leaving to join other long-tailed ducks on the seacoast long before the young hatch.

The female leads the young to water when they are about two days old. The youngsters eat insects and insect larvae, which give them the protein needed to develop flight wings. The mother teaches the young to dive, calling softly and signaling them to submerge their heads. At first, the young can only stay under water for

Top: This drake is showing off his black wings. Maybe his long tail keeps him balanced as he makes this display. *Bottom:* The long, slender tail is dark year-round and can measure up to 13 centimeters in length.

four or five seconds. But soon they will be able to stay longer, building up to their full capacity of 30, 40, and even 60 seconds.

Young become independent and can fly when they are 35 to 45 days old. Often that is the time when the ducks prepare to head south for the winter. By late August or early September, long-tailed ducks leave the breeding ground and gather in large flocks on the coast to begin their journey.

OBSERVING LONG-TAILED DUCKS

Locating a long-tailed duck can be a challenge. Unless the observer can get to the breeding grounds, he or she may have to contend with inclement weather in the winter to watch the hardy duck. The ducks winter in flocks on the Great Lakes, in large bodies of water in the west south to Nebraska and along the east and west coasts, occasionally as far south as northern California or South Carolina.

The long-tailed duck will often remain away from the harbors in the windier, colder part of the sea forcing the observer to go out a distance to find the bird. I have for four years watched flocks congregate in open water in Kenosha, Wisconsin. Finding the ducks there entails walking down a long, icy pier to a lighthouse, often amid biting wind.

Other days have been less windy and setting up a spotting scope has afforded a nice look at the seafaring ducks as they bob up and down on the waves like beach balls.

Local bird watchers, especially members of bird-watching clubs such as the Audubon Society, may provide good information on where to find long-tailed ducks in a particular area. The observer, dressed warmly, will agree that the reward is worth the effort as ducks intone their yodel-like calls and careen gregariously along the waves displaying their cheery white winter garb.

The black and white patterns of the long-tailed duck, in all of their various plumages, afford the artist a plethora of painting variations. Choose your challenge!

Mallard
(Anas platyrhynchos)

BY RICK BURKMAN

Opening pages: The drake mallard makes his entrance with wings back and head down, while calling to alert others that he's on his way in. *Above:* The mallard drake's most characteristic trait is the iridescent green head, separated from the lower neck by a distinctive white band.

Ask a child to draw a duck, and you'll probably get something with a gray or brown body and a rich green head, the familiar pattern of North America's most common waterfowl—the mallard (*Anas platyrhynchos*). Mallards are familiar because they are abundant in the wild, yet they readily adapt to man-made environments. In addition, most of the domesticated duck strains that exist today are descended from the mallard.

Because of their ubiquitous nature and their relative tameness around people, mallards have become a favorite subject for carvers, both novice and professional. Capturing the intricacies of the male's curlicue tail, the subtle vermiculation of the body feathers, and the iridescence of the brilliant head make this a challenging bird for all levels. But the fun of sculpting is not restricted to the drake alone. Carving a mallard hen is equally challenging, whether creating a realistic sculpture, a decoy, or a smoothie. Each feather is a multi-toned challenge that tests the skills of even the most experienced artisan.

APPEARANCE

The mallard's most distinguishing characteristic is the male's iridescent green head, which shimmers with bluish-purple reflections in the sunlight. A narrow white neckband separates the green head from the chestnut-colored breast. The back and abdomen are a vermiculated gray.

However, the back has a slight brownish tinge that makes it darker than the belly. The rump, upper-tail coverts, under-tail coverts, and central tail feathers are black. The central tail feathers also curl toward the back and make a little curlicue on the bird's rump. The tail edges are white and contrast sharply with the dark coverts.

The drake's wings are brownish-gray. The greater coverts are tipped with broad white bands, while the secondary coverts are a deep iridescent blue. Together the greater and secondary coverts create a distinctive shimmering blue speculum bordered with white. The underwings of the drake are lighter and brighter than the upper parts of the wings.

The overall color pattern of the drake is finished with orange legs, an olive-green to yellow-colored bill with some bluish tinges and a black tip, along with a deep brown eye.

The colors of the female, like most members of the duck family, are more subdued and cryptic. The duck is a study in earth tones, with a pleasing mix of browns, siennas, and tans. The crown, back of the neck, and eyeline are generally darker than the rest of the head.

The body is lighter and the feathers each have a distinctive dark-brown V marking. The abdomen is even paler than the rest of the body, creating a gradation of dark to light as you look from the bird's back to its belly. The tail is similar in color to the belly, and the hen lacks the drake's curlicue central tail feathers.

The wing is similar to the male's, except that it is browner overall. The speculum, like that found on the male, is deep blue bordered with white. The bill is generally a muddy orange or yellowish orange with a dark tip. The legs are orange.

Female mallards resemble several other duck species and can, at first glance, be confused with female gadwalls, mottled ducks, and black ducks. However, there are some distinguishing characteristics. Gadwalls have greenish speculums with dark borders, and black ducks are darker overall and have purple speculums with black borders.

To make identification truly confusing, mallards will regularly hybridize with other duck species, most notably black ducks, but also with gadwall, pintails, teal, wigeon, domesticated farm ducks, and others. Male hybrids have characteristics of both parent species, including a mix of feather and skin colors and changes in head shape. Female hybrids are more difficult to recognize because of their

Above right: The bill of the drake is generally a muddy orange or yellowish orange with a dark tip. *Right:* Low-headed mallards are great to include in your hunting rig for variety and to add to the appearance of a body of water that is safe for unsuspecting migrants to relax and feed.

Mallard Measurements				
	Adult Male	**Adult Female**	**Immature Male**	**Immature Female**
Length	20.4–27.5 in. Average 24.7 in.	21.7–24.7 in. Average 23.1 in.	18.4–26.0 in. Average 22.3 in.	19.8–21.5 in. Average 20.4 in.
Wing	11.4 in.	10.6 in.	11.0 in.	10.4 in.
Weight	1.5–3.8 lbs. Average 2.75 lbs.	1.2–3.8 lbs. Average 2.44 lbs.	1.2–3.6 lbs. Average 2.63 lbs.	1.1–3.7 lbs. Average 2.31 lbs.

Preening positions are a challenge for the carver and of delightful interest to the viewer. The top photo also affords a good view of the top of the drake's head.

already cryptic coloration, but they, too, will show a mix of the body types and coloration of the parent birds.

BIOLOGY

Mallard courtship begins in early fall and continues through spring. Early courtship stages are easy to miss because they are subtle and brief. Females incite male competition by stretching their heads and necks over the water and swimming near groups of drakes. The drakes respond by milling about, then rapidly shaking their heads or tails. On occasion, one of the drakes will briefly lift his head and chest out of the water and quickly drop back down. Displays become more obvious when the male birds straighten their necks, raise their tails and wing tips, and turn their heads toward the inciting female. Sometimes a competing male will lift his tail slightly out of the water, dip his bill into the water, and then abruptly lift his head to create a fine spray. These displays take place quickly, for a couple of seconds only, yet this is the beginning of courtship.

Eventually a duck and a drake pair off, leaving other suitors to test their skills elsewhere. Paired birds are relatively easy to recognize. The female follows the male, flicking her head from side to side while the male studiously leads her on. The couple strengthens its pair bond by joining in mock preening, when the birds raise wingtips over their backs, spread their wing feathers like oriental fans, and show off their brilliant blue speculum. They place their bills behind their wings, looking coy as they pretend to preen their wing feathers. Prior to mating, the birds face off, bobbing their heads up and down as they perform an age-old dance of recognition.

Nest building and incubation is strictly the female's department. She chooses a site, sometimes hundreds of meters away from the water, with some type of overhanging cover for concealment. Although typically a ground

Although mallards will fly south to escape winter conditions, they remain north as long as their habitats stay unfrozen and food is readily available. They are not especially picky about the water they use, as anyone who has seen a mallard splashing in a puddle can attest.

Mallards in flight are a common sight throughout much of North America. In this photo, the mallard's dark, chestnut-colored breast and vermiculated gray belly are on display.

Above: Following mating season, the drake will molt and lose much of his resplendence. For a month or so, the molting drake will be flightless. *Right:* Mallards are birds of leisure, and include a wealth of edibles in their diet. Insect larvae, shrimp, snails, acorns, cereal grains, and many other snackables fill their gullets.

nester, a mallard will occasionally raise a brood in a tree cavity or in an abandoned crow or raptor nest.

To construct a typical ground nest, the hen will lie on her chosen spot, dig her breast into the earth, and push herself in circles until she forms a small depression in the soil. She carries nothing to the nest, but will pull in nearby grasses, leaves, and other ground detritus to line the nest depression. To provide aerial concealment, the hen pulls grasses and nearby vegetation over her and the nest. Once she begins laying eggs, the hen plucks downy feathers from her breast and lines the nest's bottom with a soft insulating layer that protects her eggs from the cool, damp ground.

A hen lays one egg each day until she has a clutch of approximately nine. Each time she lays an egg she scrapes

a little more dirt from the nest bowl, adds a few more pieces of vegetation, and drops a few more feathers in the nest. Incubation begins while the hen lays the eggs. She spends more and more time sitting on the nest each day until, finally, she spends the majority of her time incubating with little more than a morning and afternoon break for eating, stretching, and preening.

Twenty-eight days later the eggs begin to hatch. The young birds start calling from within their shells, warning the world that a new duck brood is ready to enter the wetland community. Soon they push their way free of their shells, wet and weak from their month-long confinement. Within a few hours the ducklings dry, their musculature increases, and they start making quick forays away from the nest and back again, taking their first brave steps into the world. Within 12 hours,

Facing page: The greater coverts are tipped with broad white bands, while the secondary coverts are a deep iridescent blue. Together the greater and secondary coverts create a distinctive shimmering blue speculum bordered with white. *Top:* A mallard hen will usually lay one egg a day, for an average total of nine. As she adds to the egg count, she removes down from her breast and uses it to cushion the nest. *Bottom:* Mallard chicks are precocial, meaning they can walk, swim, and feed themselves very quickly. Within a day, the hen is leading her new brood to water.

all of the ducklings have hatched and dried. The mother leads them to nearby water to feed, grow, and begin their lives as the newest generation of ducklings.

HABITAT

Mallards are adaptable birds and their preferred habitat varies throughout their range. The population peaks where grasslands and wetlands meet in the prairie pothole region of central North America, but they thrive in any area with fresh water and enough vegetation to provide food and cover. They will find trickles of water as small as roadside ditches or as large as the Great Lakes, and pretty much anything in between, including park ponds, man-made lagoons, and woodland streams.

When grains ripen in late summer and early fall, mallards will leave their watery homes and travel inland to feed. They glean seeds from the ground and pull the heads off grasses until their crops are full, then they do what mallards enjoy best—they sleep.

BEHAVIOR

Mallards are birds of leisure. A typical day begins with feeding, usually an easy task, since mallards are not picky eaters. If it floats, burrows in the mud, sits on the ground,

The drake has moved on by the time the hen begins laying. For the most part, mallards are monogamous—but only for a single mating season. Occasionally, a drake will be seen accompanying a hen and her brood, but generally the hen is completely on her own when raising the young.

Mallard hens are also known as "susies." It is the hen that emits the loud "quack, quack" associated with mallards. The drake is the quieter of the two.

or grows on a stalk and fits in a mallard gullet, it's likely to appear on the mallard's menu. It will eat insect larvae, shrimp, snails, acorns, and cereal grains.

After the morning meal, the mallards attend to the day's cleaning. They bathe by dipping their heads in the water and splashing it along their backs. After shaking to roll off the droplets, they are ready for preening. Feather preening removes bits of debris that have worked their way into the insulating feathers, and ensures that the outer feathers are combed and oiled to protect the birds throughout the day. Then it is time for the first daytime nap. The mallard spends 65 percent of its day napping and sleeping. Like other waterfowl, the mallard will stand on one or both legs, face into the wind, tuck its bill along its back, and sleep. Interestingly, mallards can sleep with one eye open, but not always the same eye. They alternate eyes, slowly opening one to gaze for predators while the other remains closed. The edge birds in a sleeping group are more likely to exhibit this behavior than the centrally positioned birds, and the edge birds are more likely to keep their open eye away from the group's center.

RANGE/SEASON OF APPEARANCE

As summer draws to a close, mallards begin to flock together. However, this hardy bird is not preparing for an epic long-distance journey to the southern hemisphere. Instead, mallards are considered partial migrants, which means that northern birds will stay as far north as open waters allow, flying southward only when ice forces them from their homes. Even the ones that do migrate to southern climes will not stay away for long. Migrants wend their way north as soon as the ice melts and open water and food become available.

As long as they have a bit of water to swim in, a little land to nest on, and a few tidbits to eat, the ubiquitous mallard will continue to provide artists with a ready subject.

Common Merganser
(*Mergus merganser*)

BY STEVE MASLOWSKI

Opening pages: On the nesting grounds, courtship involves a variety of displays by the male. The drake may at times stretch its neck and raise up so that only its hind parts are in the water, and give a few exaggerated wing flaps and a brief call. *Above:* Common merganser hens have a distinctive chestnut-colored head and a grayish body that is darker on the back than the belly.

Winter's grasp on the northern lake has just started to loosen when, over the narrow slice of water between the rocky shore and great cake of ice covering most of the lake, a small flock of ducks flies quickly by in single file. The ducks' bold white-and-dark plumage, horizontal flight posture and low, water-skimming altitude indicate they are common mergansers. But we could predict their identity almost by season alone. Common mergansers, especially adult males, are among the earliest migrants to northern lakes and streams.

In fact, drakes, which seem particularly hardy, often haunt the edge of winter freeze-up, traveling north and south with the arrival and retreat of Arctic blasts. If rapids in a river offer open water, some common mergansers may stay in the north country all season, even though nearby lakes are ice-covered. After a while, though, their gluttonous piscatorial appetite may exhaust the rapids'

resources, and the birds will have to look for new food sources. The first line of ice-free water on a lake in early spring can be particularly attractive because fish gather there to bask in the only sunlight available in months.

In coming weeks, as the lake continues to open, increasing numbers of hens and less hardy drakes will trickle north in small groups ranging from a single pair to up to a couple dozen individuals. Unlike other waterfowl that travel in big flocks, common mergansers seem to shun crowds. The arriving mergansers will thinly, but widely, populate clear, cold freshwater lakes and rivers across a broad band of the continent. Their nesting range stretches coast to coast, mostly covering the boreal forest regions above the Great Lakes. Populations also inhabit the Rockies south to Arizona, the West Coast south to central California, Iceland, and much of Eurasia as well. The word "common" in the species' name refers to this wide global distribution, rather than to its population density. The common merganser is not fond of saltwater, and visits it only when forced to by winter ice or shortage of food.

NESTING AND DIET

On the nesting grounds, courtship involves a variety of displays by the male, including a high-speed swim that generates a significant wake. When really intense, the drake may almost run across the water, beating the surface with its wings. The drake at times may also stretch its neck and rise up so that only its hind parts are in the water, and give a few exaggerated wing flaps and a brief call.

The nesting hen uses a tree cavity, if available. This is preferably at water's edge, but may be well-recessed into the forest. The hen merganser, for all its flight speed, is surprisingly adept at threading its way through stands of trees. The day-old mergansers leap from the nest like young wood ducks, heedless of whether water or land will provide their first earthly contact. One hen merganser's nest was discovered 100 feet above the ground. There was no report about the condition of the chicks after their crash landing.

Since tree cavities are in chronically short supply for most non-woodpecker cavity nesters, mergansers often have to improvise at nesting time. In one case, four females used separate cavities in a single well-riddled tree. More often, hens end up nesting on

The drake's head may appear black in some lighting, but it is actually an iridescent green. It has a small crest that is rarely displayed.

Common Merganser Measurements				
	Adult Male	**Adult Female**	**Immature Male**	**Immature Female**
Length	23.5–27.1 in. Average 25.5 in.	21.3–26.6 in. Average 22.9 in.		
Wing	10.5 in.	9.8 in.	10.3 in.	9.5 in.
Weight	2.9–4.5 lbs. Average 3.64 lbs.	2.1–3.1 lbs. Average 2.73 lbs.	2.6–4.0 lbs. Average 3.23 lbs.	2.0–3.2 lbs. Average 2.59 lbs.

Both sexes of the common merganser are equipped with a red, thin, conical, and serrated bill for grabbing and holding their prey.

the ground. Usually they tunnel back under a thicket of low branches amid a tangle of exposed roots or into a crevice in rocks. However, in parts of Europe, concerned homeowners provide common mergansers access to attics during the nesting season. As many as four nests have been found in a single attic. In a few places, nest boxes help alleviate the housing crunch. The merganser does not seem to take to nest boxes as quickly as the wood duck, but perhaps someday nest boxes will play a more significant role for the species.

After hatching, the 10 or 12 precocious young begin eating insects. Aquatic bugs and larvae are abundant, easy to catch, and provide the enormous doses of protein and calcium needed for rapid avian growth. But within a few weeks, the chicks will start catching fish, and then remain devout fishermen for the rest of their lives.

A typical fishing trip involves a dive into about a fathom (six feet) of water, powered by feet paddling alternately or in unison. If the prey hides under a rock, the merganser can probe crevices with its narrow, serrated bill. Mergansers also like to cruise the surface with their faces submerged so they can peer better into the depths. Mergansers may dive quickly with an arcing plunge or slowly sink like a grebe.

Stream-dwelling mergansers are apt to visit swift water at dinnertime. No matter how strong the current or frothy the foam, the ducks appear to swim and dive effortlessly. Undoubtedly in rapids, where many of the swift water denizens hide from the current behind rocks,

the mergansers' willingness to probe crevices is an important asset.

In general, the species of fish the mergansers eat reflect what species are in the water. If the mergansers happen to live on a trout stream, trout will be in their diet. If salmon fry and smolt are handy, the mergansers will eat those. If rough and forage fish are abundant, the mergansers will eat their way to good citizenry by cleansing the waters of some of these. Like many fish eaters, mergansers have prodigious appetites and can easily consume a couple dozen minnows a day.

Small fish may get gulped immediately on the spot—even if they're underwater—but bigger catches usually require a trip to the surface. There, the fish is arranged for easy head-first swallowing. Fish up to about 10 inches don't seem to daunt a hungry bird. One merganser allegedly downed a 14-inch brown trout.

Should fish become scarce, mergansers resort to other protein sources, including insects, frogs, salamanders, crayfish, and even mussels and mollusks. These get consumed shell and all. Only rarely is vegetable matter included in the diet.

PLUMAGE

While the young grow in summer, the males retreat to safe, remote waters for their molt. Like so many other waterfowl, the merganser drakes want no part of child care.

When the molt is complete, the drakes wear a clean, simple pattern. The plumage vaguely resembles that of goldeneyes, but goldeneyes are not as long, slender, and large. Most of the lower body of the drake common merganser is white, as are the lower portions of the wings. The tops of the wings are black, while the back itself is mottled gray. In poor light, the head may look black as well, but the head is actually an iridescent dark green. The male's crest is small and seldom visible.

The hen has a slightly larger double crest on the back of its russet head. The head color extends halfway down the neck, where there is a sharp line separating it from the whitish remainder. The body has a gentle gray wash, slightly darker on the back than on the belly. Both sexes are equipped with a red, thin, conical, serrated bill.

Top: Drakes are particularly hardy, and often haunt the edge of winter freeze-up, traveling north and south with the arrival and retreat of Arctic blasts. *Bottom:* The common merganser's plumage vaguely resembles that of the goldeneye, but the goldeneye is not as long, slender, and large. In fact, the common merganser is the biggest of our inland ducks. Drakes average more than three and a half pounds.

Hen common mergansers have a large double crest on the back of their russet head. The head color extends halfway down the neck, where there is a sharp line separating it from the whitish remainder.

The common merganser is the biggest of our inland ducks. Drakes average more than three and a half pounds, hens a little under three pounds. By contrast, drake mallards weigh an average of two and three quarters of a pound, drake goldeneyes barely two pounds even.

As winter sets in, the drake, hen, and young mergansers begin to mingle into small groups. They travel south reluctantly. Some birds drift as far as Virginia, Tennessee, Texas, and even southern California, but the majority stay on clear water lakes and rivers farther north. Although large flocks are not the norm, at times hundreds and even thousands of common mergansers have collected on impoundments where food was especially plentiful. These big flocks are most often reported in western states.

Since the merganser's diet yields an unsavory flavor, hunting season pretty much comes and goes without effect on the species. In past eras, mergansers that happened to fly by hunters were shot at for the sheer challenge, because

Above: The word "common" in the species name refers to its wide global distribution rather than to its population density.
Right: The strength of the wings in hefting this large bird to flight is apparent in the drake's movement, with the bird straight as an arrow and intent on its destination.

their 40-plus mile per hour flight speed makes them difficult targets. Today's ethics and laws discourage such wanton killing.

Even though common mergansers are little-hunted, they remain a wary species. They are creatures of the northern wildernesses, where man has not yet intruded significantly into the rhythm of life. We may subconsciously wrinkle our noses at fish-eating ducks, but the common merganser is a hardy, well-adapted, classy-looking member of an alluring part of the world.

Hooded Merganser
(Lophodytes cucullatus)

BY CYNTHIA BERGER

Opening pages: This photo offers an excellent profile view of the hoodie's feather groups in a relaxed floating pose. *Above:* As the merganser reaches back to preen its feathers, its neck and crest extend. It's amazing how flexible a duck neck can be!

The first hooded merganser I ever saw was in a painting. I had just started work at the Cornell Lab of Ornithology, a bird research center in Ithaca, New York, and my newcomer's tour included a stop in the intimate, darkly-paneled auditorium, where a dramatic series of oil paintings by the great bird artist, Louis Agassiz Fuertes, wraps around the walls. The paintings move the viewer from one habitat to another: from open ocean to seashore, wetlands, lowlands, and mountaintop. In one wetlands panel, a lone male merganser floats quietly on the dark waters of a northern marsh. In the background are the tall spires of spruce trees and low, rounded blue hills. The merganser holds his odd, narrow black beak at a jaunty tilt, and his crest, a bulging, flamboyant pompadour with a huge, fan-shaped white spot, is startling against the austerity of the wilderness landscape. "What a strange-looking duck!" I remember thinking. "I'd love to see one."

I didn't have long to wait. The Lab of Ornithology also has a "bird observatory," a sunny room with huge windows that overlook the Sapsucker Woods Bird Sanctuary and a little pond. This pond is a magnet for waterfowl migrating through the area, so staff members drop their work and grab their binoculars whenever something interesting shows up. For me, it was the perfect crash course in duck identification. Something new seemed to touch down each day: northern pintail, wigeon, and, one day, unmistakably, a male hooded merganser.

The bird's scientific name, *Lophodytes cucullatus*, means "hooded diver," and, as I watched, the small black-and-white form sank smoothly below the surface of the pond. He reappeared a minute later some 20 yards away, tossing his head and gulping. Hooded mergansers have excellent underwater vision, thanks to specialized membranes that slide over their eyes when they dive. The ability to see underwater comes in handy because, unlike the "dabbling" ducks that strain plants from the water, hooded mergansers actively chase after their meals—mostly small fish, crayfish, and aquatic insects. Writer Christine Jerome, who admires mergansers swimming underwater in her book, *Adirondack Passage*, has a tongue-in-cheek hypothesis about the selective pressure that led to this foraging behavior. "I like to imagine," she says, "that mergansers learned to dive because they were unwilling to look as ludicrous as dabblers, who feed with their heads completely submerged and [their] fannies directed defenselessly at the sky."

HOW TO TELL A HOODIE

The spring duck parade at the Lab of Ornithology also gave me a look at the one duck you just might, at a distance, mistake for a male hooded merganser: a male bufflehead. This equally diminutive duck also has a white breast and a big white spot on its dark head; and where I live, in central New York, you often find buffleheads and hooded mergansers sharing the same stretch of water. A closer look, though, and the hoodie's dark, serrated bill can't possibly be confused with the bufflehead's classic duck bill. You'd also be unlikely to mistake the hooded merganser for either of the two other North American mergansers, the common and red-breasted; both of these are significantly larger and, in breeding plumage, the males have green heads and reddish bills. Silhouetted in flight, the hooded merganser could be mistaken for anther bird that shares its habitat: the wood duck. Both are slim with large tails and look dark above, light below.

The female hooded merganser is a drab gray-brown, darker above than below. Her crest is rusty brown, with no flamboyant white spot. I'd stared at the Fuertes merganser in the auditorium through several of the Lab's Monday-night bird seminars before I noticed the female, like a shadow,

The female is a drab gray-brown, darker above than below. Her crest is rusty-brown, with no flamboyant white spot.

Hooded Merganser Measurements				
	Adult Male	**Adult Female**	**Immature Male**	**Immature Female**
Length	17.0–19.2 in. Average 18.1 in.	16.0–18.0 in. Average 17.1 in.		
Wing	7.7 in.	7.4 in.	7.4 in.	7.2 in.
Weight	1.6 lbs.	1.5 lbs.	1.4 lbs.	1.5 lbs.

Top: The male's crest can take many forms—sometimes elongated (as in this photo) and at other times rounded or compressed. *Bottom:* The female merganser builds her down-lined nest without any help from her mate. Then she lays six to twelve round, white eggs, and raises the young alone.

hovering behind him. Females are just as inconspicuous in the field.

HABITAT AND RANGE

Like most of Fuertes' works, the painting at the Lab of Ornithology carefully places the hooded merganser in its most characteristic setting. John Phillips, in his classic 1926 book, *A Natural History of the Ducks*, says the hooded merganser "loves small, wood-enclosed waters: overflowed woods . . . and slow streams . . . . [It] also winters in the creeks and ponds of large marshes." In the most up-to-date description of this duck's natural history, the species account written for *Birds of North America*, merganser specialists Bruce and Katie Dugger and Leigh Fredrickson point out that hooded mergansers may be seen in grasslands, as well as wetlands that aren't associated with forests. But, in general, combine woods and wetness and you've got habitat for hoodies.

Unlike its larger merganser relatives, whose ranges extend to northern Europe, the hooded merganser is found only in North America. It's a bicoastal bird; in the East, hooded mergansers are especially common around the Great Lakes, though the breeding population is widely distributed from southern Canada throughout the northern and central part of the eastern United States—wherever there's suitable habitat. Meanwhile, the western population of hooded mergansers breeds in southern Alaska, parts of British Columbia, and the American northwest. These ducks are what scientists call short- to intermediate-distance migrants; eastern birds winter in the southeastern United States, and western birds winter in the Pacific Northwest north of California. They're also late-moving migrants, timing their travels to arrive on the breeding grounds just after ice-out in the spring and leave just before ice-up in the fall.

BREEDING

As you might guess, that flashy crest is the key to the male hooded merganser's appeal during courtship. With the crest folded flat, the male seems to have a small black head decorated with a thin, horizontal white streak. But when he opens the crest up to its fullest extent, he acquires a bulging pompadour that Elvis would envy. And the white streak unfolds into a conspicuous, fan-shaped white spot. Then the male shakes his head or pumps it up and down to call attention to his crowning glory. He also vocalizes. Breeding season is the one time of year when this usually quiet duck gets noisy; in some southern states, it's nicknamed the "frog duck" for its throaty call, which some people say sounds like the song of a pickerel frog.

Though this courtship ritual sounds conspicuous, mergansers are such secretive birds that it's rare to catch them in the act. Bruce Dugger, a researcher at the Archbold Biological Station, says with some bemusement that, despite all the time he's spent

Hooded mergansers have excellent underwater vision. Unlike dabbling ducks, hoodies chase and dive for their meals, feeding on small fish, crayfish, and aquatic insects.

Top: Here's an excellent view of the rear of the head and body feathers of the common merganser. *Bottom:* Great catch! Now the only question is how to get it down!

in the woods, he has never seen the display in the wild, only in videos. "That's how hard it is to see these ducks," he says.

Like the more familiar wood ducks, hooded mergansers are cavity-nesters who will accept a nest box when hollow trees are in short supply. Leigh Fredrickson has studied hooded mergansers for 35 years at the University of Missouri-Columbia, and he's fascinated by the way these two species share the same patch of woods. "Wood ducks breed at one year old; hooded mergansers don't mature till they're two," he says. "But mergansers tend to nest earlier in the spring, so they get first access to nest cavities, before the wood ducks. On the other hand, if a wood duck is successful in a nest site, there's a high likelihood it will come back to the same spot next year. The mergansers do come back to the same general area, but not to the exact same nest site."

The female merganser builds her down-lined nest without any help from her mate. Then she lays one egg every other day, till she has a clutch of six to twelve. But she may end up incubating many more, because hooded mergansers are "dump-nesters." A female who can't find a suitable nest site of her own often sneaks into another hoodie's nest to lay her eggs. This dump-nesting even crosses species lines: hooded mergansers may leave their eggs in the nests of wood ducks, common goldeneyes, and common mergansers, and they may end up incubating the eggs of any of these species.

Hooded merganser eggs are unusual. They're round instead of "egg-shaped," and they have very thick shells. In a letter to the venerable bird writer Arthur Cleveland Bent (author of the series commonly referred to as *Bent's Life Histories*), one writer described these eggs as being "just about the size, shape, and color of white billiard balls—and every bit as hard."

Though courtship rituals are loud and flashy, mergansers are such secretive birds that you'll rarely, if ever, catch them in the act.

After the female starts incubating the eggs, the male abandons her. Where he goes is something of a mystery, according to Leigh Fredrickson. "They simply disappear halfway through the incubation period, and we don't see them again till fall," he says. Through tagging studies, Fredrickson has collected some evidence that male mergansers in Missouri are moving farther north, to North Dakota and Minnesota. One possible explanation for this breeding-season dispersal is that males find more food on the prairies so they avoid competing with the females and young for limited resources.

CONSERVATION CONCERNS

The plight of migratory birds is a hot topic in conservation circles. So how's the hooded merganser doing? It's hard to get a handle on hoodie numbers, says Bruce Dugger. "Most bird population survey techniques assume that the birds are concentrated in a place where they're easy to see and easy to capture," he says. "But that doesn't happen with hooded mergansers. They prefer heavily forested habitats. It's very unusual to see flocks of more than 20 or 30 birds. So a survey that's effective for prairie-nesting ducks doesn't work for mergansers."

Making their best estimates from available data, however, waterfowl experts agree that hooded merganser numbers seem to be holding steady and even increasing in some locations. But before we feel too complacent, consider that these secretive birds leave scientists with plenty to study: for example, exactly what habitats they prefer and why, how habitat alterations, such as logging, affect them, and whether hunting is taking a toll on populations. Another concern is heavy metal contamination of their habitat, which is especially common in the Great Lakes region. Maybe part of the hooded merganser's mystique is that there's much to be discovered—especially if you like things wet and wild.

Red–breasted Merganser
(Mergus serrator)

BY RICK BURKMAN

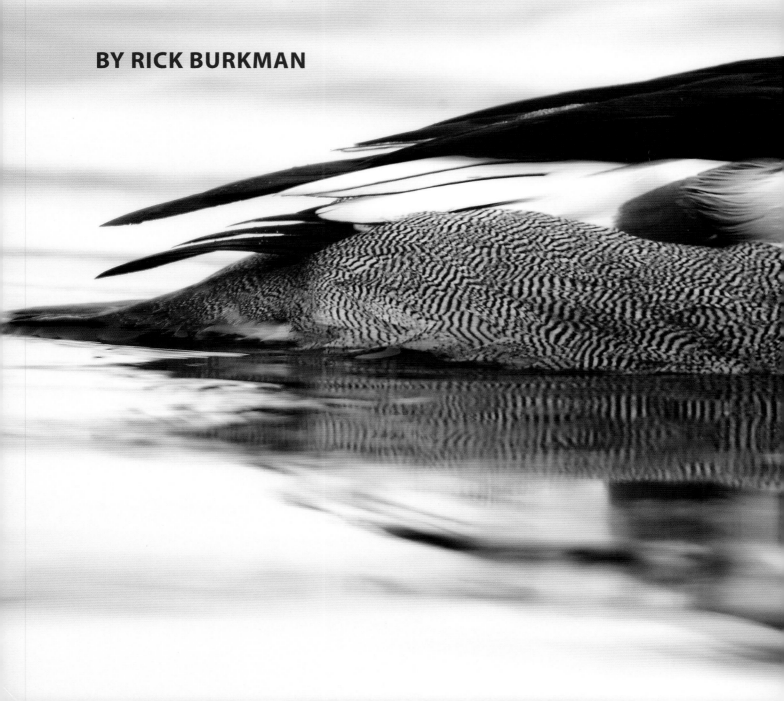

There are few sights in nature more entertaining than the hunting antics of the red-breasted merganser. These ducks with unruly crests swim with their bodies on the water's surface and their faces stuck under the waves like periscopes in reverse as they search for silvery minnows, tadpoles, crayfish, and other aquatic prey. When they spot their quarry, the mergansers execute smooth, looping dives that barely ripple the water's surface, and the hunt is on.

Their strong, dark red feet and legs are placed well back on their bodies, making them clumsy and uncomfortable on land, but smooth and lithe in their preferred cool, wet water world. They use their paddle-like feet to dart after prey, executing pinpoint turns as they chase small darting fish. The chase is propelled entirely by their feet, with their wings held tightly to their bodies.

Opening pages: Wow! This is the postcard view of the red-breasted merganser in all its glory, as it glides regally through the water with its crest fully extended. *Top:* The female red-breasted merganser's head and neck are paler than those of the female common merganser. Her chin and foreneck are white, and her white inner secondaries and greater coverts are crossed by a single black bar. *Bottom:* The red-breasted merganser drake can be distinguished from the common merganser by its shaggy double crest, white collar, and streaked breast.

Modified lamellae, the hard comb-like "teeth" that line their bills, help them hold slippery, struggling prey. Still, this world belongs to the fish, and the merganser successfully captures its prey less than ten percent of the time. Small fish are their preferred food, but they are also happy poking and probing their long, thin bills into the cracks and crevices of logs and rocks, hoping to bump into unsuspecting crawfish or dragonfly larvae.

BREEDING AND NESTING

Red-breasted mergansers are social within their own species, and it is common to find them grouped into hunting packs, small flocks working in well-orchestrated concert to herd and concentrate minnows. At some predetermined moment known only to the ducks, they dive together to capture the corralled fish.

Working in groups extends to the birds' breeding season. Several males may follow and cajole a single female in the hope of attracting her attention. The males, resplendent with their velvety black and deep green heads, will extend their necks to expose their white throats, rusty breasts and piercing red eyes. The neck stretch is followed by a curtsy, in which the head

The red-breasted's strong, dark-red feet and legs are placed well back on its body, making it clumsy and uncomfortable on land but smooth and lithe in its preferred cool, wet, water world.

Red-breasted Merganser Measurements				
	Adult Male	**Adult Female**	**Immature Male**	**Immature Female**
Length	16.1–18.1 in. Average 17.1 in.	16.0–16.6 in. Average 17.1 in.	16.0–16.6 in. Average 17.5 in.	16.2–18.6 in. Average 17.1 in.
Wing	9.5 in.	8.7 in.	9.1 in.	8.4 in.
Weight	1.4–1.8 lbs. Average 1.56 lbs.	1.3–1.7 lbs. Average 1.52 lbs.	1.6–1.9 lbs. Average 1.76 lbs.	1.4–1.8 lbs. Average 1.63 lbs.

and tail are tilted upward and the chest and abdomen are pushed down into the water. Like synchronized swimmers, several males will paddle in front of a potential mate, performing their dance in unison. After this dramatic display, the birds return to a normal swimming posture, with their double crest trailing behind them. Eventually, the female becomes receptive to one or more of the courting males, and copulation occurs. DNA testing has shown that a clutch of eggs is generally fertilized by more than one male.

After mating, it is time for the female to make a nest, a process that requires little time and effort. She prepares a small scrape in the ground, usually under a dense canopy of grasses, rushes, or shrubs and always within sight of the water. Sometimes the scrape is placed under an old log or a pile of weathered driftwood. One was even found in an abandoned igloo. The female does not line the scrape, but, after incubation begins, she pulls grasses and other vegetation from nearby into the nest. Feathers pulled from her breast add a small amount of insulation to the eggs. Several females may nest in the same area, and the mergansers will also nest close to other colonial birds like gulls and terns.

A light beige or light gray egg is laid every one and a half days until a clutch of nine or ten eggs is completed. There have been nests with up to 56 eggs discovered—quite an accomplishment since each egg laid equals about seven percent of the female's total body weight. Nests of that size are

Top: Modified lamellae, the hard comb-like "teeth" that line the mergansers' bills, help the birds hold slippery, struggling prey. *Bottom:* It's a stretch to reach those tail feathers, but this merganser is determined!

likely the result of "egg-dumping," a poorly understood process in which several females will lay eggs in a single nest. The females do not discriminate when dumping their eggs. Red-breasted merganser eggs have been found in the nests of Barrow's goldeneyes, harlequin ducks, mallards, scaups, gadwalls, and gulls.

YOUNG LIFE

The parental duties of the males end when incubation begins. After about a month of incubation, the first signs of hatching occur. Tapping sounds come from inside the eggs. Soon, small peeping sounds are heard as the ducklings, still in their shells, begin to communicate with the outside world. It is believed that the peeping helps to synchronize the hatching process so that all of the young birds break free of their shells at about the same time. On

Top: In the United States, this species winters primarily along the Atlantic, Gulf, and Pacific coasts, with the highest numbers found along the Atlantic flyway. *Bottom:* The drake's head is iridescent green, and the breast is rusty brown with black specks. The bill is scarlet-orange.

This species lays approximately ten olive-buff eggs to each clutch. The elliptical eggs typically measure 64½ by 45 millimeters.

hatching day, the ducklings break out of their shells wet, bedraggled, and weak. They stay under the warm outstretched wings of the female for a few hours as their downy plumage dries. They quickly gain strength and soon the downy balls of grayish brown fluff venture forth, never intentionally returning to their hatching spot.

Their mother leads them to the water, where they instinctively begin swimming and pecking at bugs, larvae, and various tiny invertebrates. Some ducks are excellent mothers, brooding their young during stormy weather and leading them away from danger, while other females abandon their young to the care of creche mothers soon after leading them to water. The creche mothers may lead several broods at one time. There is even one recorded instance of a brood mother caring for about 100 ducklings before other "aunties" stepped in to lighten the burden.

Both genetic mothers and creche hens will brood the young during periods of bad weather for the first two weeks of life, but after that the young birds fend for themselves more and more often. They are well adapted to bo-

real life, and, if there are too many ducklings for the hen to brood at one time, the young will more quickly gain the ability to maintain their body temperature even on the coldest days.

The parental bond does not stay strong for very long. After about seven weeks, well before the youngsters can fly, their caretaker abandons them, leaving the young birds to fend for themselves. If all goes well, the young birds will survive through their juvenile period and live into adulthood. When capable of flying, they will join loose flocks and travel south for the winter.

Although it takes some effort for mergansers to become airborne, once in flight, they can travel at speeds of up to 80 miles per hour. They move south, barely keeping ahead of the oncoming winter until they reach their winter homes along the southern Great Lakes shoreline or along the Atlantic and Pacific seashores. When spring arrives, they will once again take to the air and journey northward to add a splash of beauty to the coolness of the world's boreal forests.

Northern Pintail
(*Anas Acuta*)

BY DR. ROBERT I. SMITH

Opening pages: The pintail's streamlined body is designed for flying. Migrations take pintails from the Arctic to Mexico and from Alaska to the South Pacific. *Above:* A long, slender neck, distinctive head shape, and tail feathers that make up a full one-quarter of its total body length give the pintail an elegant, graceful look.

The pintail, also known as sprig, is one of the largest dabbling ducks. Found throughout the northern hemisphere, the pintail predominates in the western part of the United States, yet it still has far-ranging appeal as a subject for carvings and paintings.

A long, slender neck, distinctive head shape, and tail feathers that make up a full one-quarter of its total body length give the pintail an elegant, graceful look. Some describe the drake as having a royal air about him. The shape of the bill also adds to its regal appearance. The upper surface of the bill slopes rather sharply downward from the skull to a nearly flat area about halfway from the tip.

Like most avian species, the drake's plumage immediately distinguishes it from any other species. In contrast, the hen's plumage tends to appear similar to that of other dabbling duck hens. The pintail drake in breeding plumage has chocolate brown and white plumage arranged in striking contrast, making it one of the most beautiful ducks. The two long, central tail feathers for which the species is named are black, while the other tail feathers are gray with white trim. The hen's plumage can range from brown to a gray that contains only a hint of brown.

Dabbling ducks feed in shallow water. On a scale of one to ten, with shallow water at one and deep water at ten, the pintail prefers feeding at one. The pintail feels at home when both feet are planted firmly on the ground while it excavates soil with its bill. In some situations, pintails feed in moist soil where there is no standing water. Its bill is designed for probing into moist soil for tubers, seeds and invertebrates. The bill of the drake is light blue and black. During the non-breeding season, these bill colors fade to shades of gray.

The typical setting for a pintail at rest is not a beaver pond or a stand of cattails but a bed of spikerush that is no more than five to ten inches high. This setting occurs in the Arctic, in the mountain valleys of the West, in shallow ponds on the prairies, and on tidal flats. In short, the pintail prefers open spaces.

MIGRATION AND BREEDING

The streamlined body of a pintail is designed for flying. Migrations take pintails from the Arctic to Mexico and from Alaska to the South Pacific. Pintails migrate from the steppes of Asia to the delta of the Nile. Tombs of ancient pharaohs contain paintings of pintails. Pintails have a tendency to return to their breeding areas using circuitous migrations; migratory pathways in the spring differ from those used in the fall. Pintail migrations never fully terminate on wintering areas, as flocks drift from one location to another in a circular pattern. Mexico, California, Texas, and Louisiana are locations where most pintails in North America can be found in winter.

Pintails are dabblers who prefer very shallow water. They like to stand along the edge of the water or in shallows while excavating the moist soil for tubers, seeds, and invertebrates.

Northern Pintail Measurements				
	Adult Male	**Adult Female**	**Immature Male**	**Immature Female**
Length	23.6–30.1 in. Average 25.2 in.	20.6–24.8 in. Average 21.4 in.	21.7–26.9 in. Average 23.9 in.	20.0–22.5 in. Average 20.4 in.
Wing	10.7 in.	10.1 in.	10.5 in.	9.8 in.
Weight	1.4–3.2 lbs. Average 2.26 lbs.	1.3–2.6 lbs. Average 1.91 lbs.	1.1–2.9 lbs. Average 2.09 lb.s	1.1–2.6 lbs. Average 1.76 lbs.

Pintails avoid strong attachments to particular locations, choosing to drift from one location to another, and using circuitous, varying migration routes.

The Canadian provinces of Alberta and Saskatchewan serve as primary nesting areas for pintails. When water is scarce on the prairies and parklands of these provinces, the pintail moves northward to the Northwest Territories and Alaska. It seems likely that a few move into Siberia as well. In the summer, as in the winter, this species avoids strong attachments to particular locations. As with most duck species, there are more pintail drakes than hens. The reason for extra drakes appears to be deaths of hens during nesting. Nesting and brood-rearing take their toll, as hens become vulnerable to predators. Pintail drakes and hens have a tendency to flock separately in the fall and early winter. It is not unusual to find a flock of 15 or 20 hens without a drake or a flock of 50 to 100 drakes without a hen. This separation is not complete, but the mixing of sexes is certainly not random.

A more obvious mixing of sexes begins in winter, and it signals the beginning of mate selection and courtship. Even mixed flocks, however, will be 65 to 75 percent drakes in late winter. The integration of males and females into flocks of pairs with more balanced sex ratios continues throughout the spring migration. This long integration process probably occurs because hens tend to winter farther south than many of the drakes and are slower to move northward in late winter. Sex ratios never become equal, and pintail flocks arrive on breeding areas in April with many unmated drakes, but unmated hens are very rare.

Facing page: This photo gives an excellent front view of the pintail, highlighting its head and wing shapes, body outline, eye placement, and white breast markings.

Above left: The upper parts of the drake are brownish to grayish with broad dark barring. The central tail feathers are brown and long, but are much shorter and wider than in breeding plumage. *Left:* Here is a view of the white stripes on the head from the rear, and a good look at the back, wing, and tail feathers. *Above right:* The crown and face of the hen pintail are tan, with a whitish chin. The back and rump are brown with lighter edges to the feathers, and the upper breast is buff.

COURTING DISPLAYS

The pintail hen attracts the attention of courting males by showing preference for a particular drake. In effect, a pintail courting party consists of a hen, a drake she prefers, and four to ten additional drakes displaying in the vicinity of this pair. Each of the three roles described above has its distinctive displays. Rarely is the preferred drake replaced by another drake during courtship, and this raises questions about the primary function of this activity among pintails. Remember, there are not enough hens to provide all drakes with a mate. Courtship no doubt has several functions, but I suggest that it provides extra males an opportunity to express their sexual intention in a manner that is less disruptive than fighting over scarce hens. Fighting among birds is of questionable benefit because it damages feathers required for flying.

The hen indicates her preference for a particular drake by moving behind him and making rhythmic motions with the head and bill along the side of her body. The preferred drake performs a display that involves raising the

As with most duck species, there are more drakes than hens. Perhaps because of the abundance of drakes, pintail hens will select a preferred mate, but they will also engage in "three-bird flights" that end with copulation with a drake other than her mate.

head upward and giving a "whee" with rising inflection, then a whistle, then lowering the head, and giving a "whee" with declining inflection. Feathers on the top of the head are erected, giving a fuller, rounder shape to the head. This display, usually performed at the side of the hen, concludes when the drake moves in front of her and displays the back of his head. Feathers on the back of the head and neck are held erect during this display.

The drakes not preferred stay at a greater distance from the hen, and they perform other displays, either on the water or in the air. One of these displays is a highly ritualized drinking or bill-cleaning movement that splashes water in the direction of the hen. Another display features the tail and the head lifted upward. All of the above occurs on water, but an aerial version of this courting activity can be seen. The aerial version seems to be triggered when the

hen and the preferred drake are losing control of the situation. In other words, the space between the pair and the extra drakes has been reduced to an unacceptable distance. If a preferred drake is to be displaced, it will likely occur in this situation.

Pintails select wetlands that are shallow and of a temporary nature, so reproduction must occur quickly if it is to be successful. The pintail lays a small clutch of eggs, perhaps as few as three. (Egg color ranges from a grayish-cream color to pale olive green.) The incubation period is relatively short—only 22–23 days—as is the interval between hatching and fledging.

During the nesting season drakes other than the mate of the hen sometimes fertilize her eggs. This promiscuous behavior is not unique to pintails, but no other duck species has such a high rate of promiscuous copulations. These cop-

The Northern pintail is among the earliest nesting ducks in North America, beginning shortly after ice-out in many northern areas.

ulations are associated with flights that differ from courtship flights. Hens ready to lay eggs exhibit a strong tendency to fly when in the presence of a drake other than their mate. These flights have been referred to as *three-bird flights* because the performers are a hen, the mate of a neighboring hen, and the drake of the hen in flight. Other drakes can join in, but they are not key players in this drama. These flights come to the ground, and more frequently than not, they terminate in promiscuous copulation.

The significance of this behavior is not clear; however, these flights, whether terminating in copulation or not, force hens to move away from neighboring hens at the time nests are initiated. One could speculate that this activity spaces nests some distance apart, thus discouraging predators from searching for and killing hens on nests.

Observations of the pintail are filled with surprises, and there are many unanswered questions regarding this species. I hope that I have conveyed enough in this brief summary to stimulate your interest.

Redhead
(*Aythya americana*)

BY SHERYL DE VORE

Opening pages: A drake redhead emerges from the mist like a vision. *Above:* A classic profile view shows the redhead's rounded head and steep forehead. Note the vermiculation, the delicate feather patterns on the side and back.

It's coppery red, writes ornithologist Paul A. Johnsgard. Others concede that it's brick red, while another writer views it as chestnut-colored. Still another sees red-brown. The descriptions of the head color of the handsome redhead, a North American diving duck, vary. But most would agree that this species proves that the colors of nature are often indescribable, offering a challenge to the carver to recreate the distinctive hue.

The redhead, *Aythya americana,* typically spends its entire life in the Northern hemisphere and is rarely found elsewhere. The redhead summers and nests in freshwater marshes of western United States and Canada east to Pennsylvania. Flocks of redheads migrate southward and eastward in fast, V-shaped flocks to winter on the Gulf, Pacific and Atlantic coasts of southern United States, Mexico, and the West Indies. The redhead may also frequent large inland bodies of water in winter.

IDENTIFICATION

Many bird watchers discover redheads gathered in large flocks for safety on inland lakes. There, observers may also see a flock of canvasbacks, which often associate with and can be mistaken for redheads since their heads are a similar color.

Observing head shape helps distinguish the two ducks. The redhead has a rounded head with a steep forehead that joins the bill at an angle. Both male and female can be identified this way. The canvasback's head slopes toward the bill forming a continuous concave line. Closer observation also helps differentiate between the birds' irises and bills. The male redhead sports a yellow iris and a blue bill tipped with white and black, while the male canvasback has a brown iris and a black bill.

In flight, male redheads look grayish white except for the black back. A broad gray wing stripe is also visible. The redhead flies deftly with strong, quick wing beats.

The male redhead sits fairly low in the water, sporting his red head and neck contrasted by a black breast and rear, which sandwich a grayish white body. With the aid of a spotting scope, the bird watcher can also see a dark line where the head meets the blue bill and a white line that meets the black tip of the bill. The female redhead's bill is similar, but her body, like the eclipse male, is brown with some white on the rear.

A medium-sized diving duck, the redhead weighs about two pounds and measures 19–20 inches long. Its wings span up to 35 inches.

COURTSHIP

As with most diving ducks, redheads are silent except during pair bonding and courtship. Since redheads begin pair bonding in early winter, those people living in the birds' non-breeding grounds may have a chance to witness the courtship rituals and hear the unusual calls of the males.

The male redhead begins his overtures to one or more females by mimicking a cat. He throws his head back and utters a loud "meow" or a purr-like sound. He may also utter softer coughing-like sounds to attract the female.

Both sexes boldly stretch their necks while forming pairs. The female responds by moving her chin from side to side and up and down. The male may respond back by swimming ahead and then turning his head back to the female as if to make sure she's still there.

Bill and eye color are two features that distinguish the redhead drake from the canvasback. The redhead has a yellow iris and white-tipped blue bill while the canvasback's iris is brown and its bill is black.

Redhead Measurements				
	Adult Male	**Adult Female**	**Immature Male**	**Immature Female**
Length	18.1–21.7 in. Average 20.0 in.	18.0–20.5 in. Average 19.0 in.		
Wing	Average 9.16 in.	Average 8.79 in.	Average 9.01 in.	Average 8.64 in.
Weight	2.1–3.2 lbs. Average 2.44 lbs.	1.5–2.0 lbs. Average 2.14 lbs.	1.4–3.0 lbs. Average 2.11 lbs.	1.4–2.8 lbs. Average 1.91 lbs.

Aerial chases in which one red-head actually pulls the tail of another can also be observed but are most typically seen once the species has reached its breeding grounds. There, the male alternately dips his bill then preens his dorsal before mounting the female.

The female builds a deep-cupped nest of reeds and her down on a mass of wetland plants such as cattails or bulrushes. Prairie potholes of an acre or more are often selected breeding

Left: The redhead sits a little lower in the water than the canvasback does. *Below:* A drake enjoys a meal of pond weeds. Redheads eat primarily vegetative matter but will also sample insects and aquatic invertebrates. *Facing page:* A small flock of redheads enjoy a tranquil moment. Redheads frequent ponds and small lakes and will intermingle with other species.

Top: A front view demonstrates the head shape. Note how the cheek tapers into the eye channel. *Above:* A fanning drake reveals his wing structure and coloring. The broad gray band is characteristic.

sites of redheads. A typical nest in Minnesota would be built in wet, emergent vegetation about 20 to 40 inches tall.

Redhead females commonly lay an average of 10 creamy-white eggs. Some may parasitize other duck nests before laying their own clutch. Still others lay their eggs in other nests and never build their own. Up to 30 redhead eggs have been found in a canvasback's nest, according to *The Audubon Society Encyclopedia of North American Birds* by John K. Terres.

When the clutch is complete, the redhead incubates the eggs about 29 days. The male may remain for a few days but usually leaves long before his young are hatched. Nestlings are an overall pale yellow with a buff tint on the face and a brownish color on the back of the neck and head. Their feet, legs, and bill are dark brown.

The ducklings remain in the nest for just a few days after which time their mother leads them out to learn to feed. Feeding is typically done in the morning and evening and sometimes even at night.

The young watch as their mother dives up to 10 feet below the surface to snatch seeds of pondweeds, wild rice, wild celery, bulrushes, and other vegetative matter. Especially during nesting, the redhead will also feed on grasshoppers and aquatic invertebrates such as mollusks for the high protein content. The redhead may also skim for duckweed on the water's surface.

The young fledge when they are between 56 and 73 days old. Then they begin to congregate in flocks as they await their first migration. Meanwhile, some of their fathers may have flown further north to molt and then prepare for their fall journey.

STATUS

Some bird watchers have noted that they don't seem to be seeing as many redheads during migration as they have in the past. Indeed, several field

Cold, snow, and ice are not the redheads' preferred conditions. Most of the birds migrate to warmer winter climates although some of them do remain behind and withstand the season's chill.

guide editions of the 1980s indicate that the redhead's numbers are declining. "This beautiful duck has suffered greatly from hunting and the destruction of its habitat; it has declined in numbers until it is one of the least common North American ducks," according to *The Audubon Society Field Guide to North American Birds* (1985 edition).

The redhead is losing its nesting sites as prairie potholes and wetlands throughout America are being destroyed. Controlled hunting as well as the re-creation of nesting habitats is helping.

For instance, the Wisconsin Department of Natural Resources, working with the United States Fish and Wildlife Services, has helped bring the redhead back to Horicon Marsh in southern Wisconsin. The 31,000-acre marsh

had virtually been destroyed when it was drained for farming in the early 1900s. In 1941, the DNR and USFS bought and revitalized the marsh to encourage redheads and other wildlife to nest there.

Each spring, Horicon Marsh visitors can now catch a glimpse of the handsome, rusty-headed duck feeding in the impoundments at the north end of the marsh. Horicon now has one of the largest nesting populations of redheads in the eastern part of their range.

A group of redheads on an inland lake during fall migration adds to the tapestry of autumn colors that surely follows every summer. As long as we continue to protect the redhead's habitat, we can also continue to enjoy its beautifully colored head and equally striking courtship behavior.

Ring-necked Duck
(Aythya colaris)

BY SHERYL DE VORE

Opening pages: What ring? The cinnamon-colored feature that gives this duck its name is actually not terribly obvious. *Above:* The white ring around the black-tipped bill is prominent on both the hen and the drake. The drake, however, has a bluish-gray bill and a white outline between the bill and the head.

Someone seeing a ring-necked duck for the first time might remark, "What an odd name. I don't see a ring around the neck." Indeed, the muted, narrow cinnamon ring on the breeding male's black neck is difficult to discern even at close range.

"Ring-billed duck," which the species is sometimes called, seems more appropriate since observers can more easily spot the white bar or ring around the black-tipped bill of the breeding male and female. Although it's considered a diving duck, *Aythya colaris* frequents habitats such as freshwater marshes, woodland ponds, and small lakes where surface-feeding, or dabbling, ducks are found. The handsome appearance of the ring-neck along with its dabbling duck habits makes it a fascinating bird to observe.

WINTERING AND BREEDING GROUNDS

In winter, ring-necks feed in the inner estuaries or brackish waters in Florida, Mexico, and the West Indies. Ring-necks also winter in small numbers from New Jersey to North Carolina and in California. These mid-season migrants begin leaving their wintering grounds in early February, traveling in train-like flocks of 20 to 60 to their breeding grounds. They nest in the boreal and temperate zones of Canada, Washington, the Dakotas, Minnesota, Wisconsin, Michigan's Upper Peninsula and Maine. The species has also expanded its breeding range to Alaska, according to John Gooders, author of *Ducks of North America.*

STATELY APPEARANCE

The observer spotting a ring-neck during migration or during its stay on breeding grounds will notice the peaked head created by long, partially raised crown feathers, which gives the duck a stately, proud appearance.

The adult male measures an average of 16 to 18 inches in length from bill tip to tail end. The breeding male has a glossy black breast, neck, head, and back with a grayish white body. The neck and head are tinged with purple reflections. A white, vertical crescent separates the chest from the flanks.

The ringed bill is bluish-gray except at the tip, which is black. A thin white line outlining the area between the bill and the black head also helps identify the male of this species.

The smaller female, averaging 15 to 17 inches in length, has a chocolate brown body with a darker brown back. Her muted brown head is also slightly peaked like the male's. The female ring-neck shows a complete white eye ring. Often, a pale white curving line extends backward from the ring. Whitewash where the bill and head meet can make the female

Although a diver, the ring-necked duck sits high on the water like a dabbler. It has powerful feet and can dive up to six feet. On the surface the drake's distinctive crown feathers contribute an air of stateliness. A white, vertical crescent separates chest from flanks.

Ring-necked Duck Measurements				
	Adult Male	**Adult Female**	**Immature Male**	**Immature Female**
Length	16.1–18.3 in. Average 17.2 in.	15.6–17.5 in. Average 16.6 in.	16.1–18.1 in. Average 17.0 in.	15.6–17.5 in. Average 16.4 in.
Wing	7.99 in.	7.64 in.	7.96 in.	7.52 in.
Weight	1.3–2.0 lbs. Average 1.64 lbs.	1.2–2.0 lbs. Average 1.48 lbs.	1.2–2.0 lbs. Average 1.56 lbs.	1.1–2.0 lbs. Average 1.50 lbs.

ring-neck look like a female scaup. Ring-necks can be confused with scaups especially at a distance. To separate the species, note the much darker black back of the adult male ring-neck. Scaups lack the ringed bills. Also scaups tend to gather in much larger groups than do ring-necks. The observer will typically see a flock of up to 20 ring-necks associating with a flock of 50 to 100 or more scaups.

In flight, ring-necks have dark wings, while scaups have single white bars on their wings. Wings of the male ring-neck typically measure eight inches in length from the bend to the tip of the longest flight feather. Wings of the female are slightly shorter.

In the water, ring-necks often display characteristics that link them with surface feeding, or dabbling ducks. They sit high on the water's surface, dabble for food, and even occasionally

Top: The hen has a complete white eye ring. Sometimes the line extends backwards from the ring. *Above:* One of a ring-neck trio displays its fine rear profile. *Facing page:* The ring-neck drake has a grayish-white body and a glossy black breast, back, and head.

Top: The drake ring-neck is more faithful than the average diver, remaining with the hen into the fourth week of incubation. *Above:* The hen has a chocolate-brown body, with darker brown on the back. The belly is white.

lift their tails in the air like mallards to get at the pond weeds, tubers, and other vegetative matter they eat.

PAIR BONDING

Bird watchers enjoying ring-neck feeding antics may not get a chance to observe courtship unless they live near the duck's breeding grounds. The male often saves his subtle overtures for springtime or his arrival on breeding grounds. To attract a female, the male raises his head, erecting his long crown feathers. He then produces a sound much like air being blown through a hollow tube. The female may pay no attention to him at first but will later respond with a soft, low-pitched purr.

Once a pair is formed, the male remains faithful well into the fourth week of incubation, an unusual occurrence for diving ducks. The female swims the border of a marsh while the male follows. While she carefully explores the marsh vegetation where

The secondary wing feathers on drakes and hens are pearl gray with dusky tips and faintly white edges. The drake's tertials are greenish black; hen's are more greenish brown. The male's wings measure about eight inches from the bend to the tip of the longest flight feather. Females' are slightly shorter.

she will make her nest, the male remains in the open water nearby. The female selects her nest site on floating clumps of marsh vegetation and sometimes on nearby islands. She prefers sedges and leather leaf.

To make her nest, the female flattens a few plants. She immediately begins to lay her nine elliptical olive-buff eggs, one each day. She periodically adds her down and sometimes weaves overhead plants to form a canopy.

In about 26 days, the first duckling pecks its way through the shell. The downy young of this species is yellow with a thin brown line curving at the tip of the head down to the neck. The juvenile back is brown splotched with yellow.

When all eggs have hatched, the female leads the young to water and will feign injury to lead away predators. Atypical of diving ducks, the female ring-neck will also often lead her young to the safety of floating islands of vegetation to avoid danger.

The young are agile divers almost immediately, but they feed by dabbling on the surface at first and advance to diving for breakfast when they are about half grown. Ring-necks dive with tightly closed wings, swimming rapidly below the surface using their powerful feet. They dive for vegetable matter as well as snails, crabs, and other aquatic animals.

After breeding season, ring-necks generally disperse on marshes, bogs, lakes, and ponds and prepare for fall migration, which can be an exciting time to observe this species. In his book, *Ducks, Geese and Swans of North America*, Frank C. Bellrose observed ring-necks leaving Maine one year. The ducks were feeding intermittently and "often rising and circling the marsh fairly high in flocks of 25 to 50 . . . . About half an hour before sunset, approximately 75 birds rose from the largest of the resting flocks, circled the lake twice at an elevation in excess of 500 feet, rose even higher, then disappeared beyond the valley in a straight line, heading due southwest."

The ring-neck flies swiftly and vigorously in tight teal-like flocks. When a flock of ring-necks bounds from the water, the observer can sometimes hear whistling sounds from its wings.

The same excitement of fall migration can also be witnessed in the spring. Driving along a one-lane highway in late April in Michigan's upper peninsula, I came upon a flock of about 15 male and female ring-necked ducks swimming in a shallow bog of cinnamon-colored Labrador tea. Ring-necked ducks had been seen a month earlier farther south in Illinois associating with scaups and buffleheads in small lakes and marshes.

Perhaps these ring-necks were the same ones seen earlier in Illinois and had now arrived at their breeding grounds. I wondered whether I would have the rare chance to witness pair bonding. But giving their one-pitched, hollow alarm call, the ring-necks slipped into the shadows, holding their crested heads high as they left.

Ruddy Duck
(*Oxyura jamaicensis*)

BY ARTHUR MORRIS

Opening pages: The ruddy duck sometimes uses its stiff tail as a rudder when swimming underwater. On the surface the tail may lie flat on the water or stick up in the air. *Above:* A courting drake creates a scene for a watching hen.

The drake gadwall popped up from the water with a beak full of algae scooped from the bottom of the East Pond and swallowed as he swam, gooey green stuff streaming from his beak. A female ruddy duck, riding shotgun on the gadwall, rapidly overtook him and grabbed tiny bits of algae right from his beak. As he paddled away, bits of algae dripped into the pond where they were quickly snatched up by the bold ruddy.

Ruddy ducks, however, are not always so brazen. I've seen them skitter across the surface in sheer panic when a group of double-crested cormorants peacefully submarined by in search of a fish dinner. This situation is even more comical when the ruddies are spooked in mid-dive!

These scenarios all took place at the Jamaica Bay Wildlife Refuge in Queens, New York, where I have spent hundreds of hours observing and photographing ruddy ducks from the permanent "East Garden" blind. Although ruddy ducks no longer breed at Jamaica Bay, hundreds stop at the refuge in March and April on the way to their breeding grounds to the north and northwest. On southbound migration, they arrive in late August and September and remain (in most years) until cold weather forces them south.

The ruddy duck (*Oxyura jamaicensis*) is a small, chunky diving duck with a thick neck and relatively large, flat bill. Its relatively long, stiff tail is often held flat on the water. At other times, it is held above the water and cocked at an angle (usually by males).

At the height of breeding plumage, male ruddy ducks are spectacularly handsome. These drakes, slightly larger than the hens, sport a rich, reddish-chestnut feathering. A large, pure white cheek patch is set off by a jet-black cap and nape. At times, the black extends to encircle the neck, creating a black-hooded effect. Their bills are an incredibly bright powder blue. In *Life Histories of North American Wild Fowl*, A. C. Bent writes of the ruddy's "wonderful bill of the brightest, living, glowing sky blue."

Unlike many other brightly colored male ducks, male ruddies do not have an eclipse plumage. Drake ruddy ducks molt directly into winter plumage during late summer to early fall. Winter males are dark brown above with black vermiculation. The cap is blackish-brown and the nape is grayish-brown. The large, white cheek patch is prominent, but duller than in spring. The neck, and at times the breast and the sides of the breast, are also grayish-brown. The flanks are a contrasting brownish-gray with blackish-brown vermiculation. The bill varies from dark gray to black. Overall, winter males are far duller than breeding-plumaged males.

Winter-plumaged females and first-year (immature) birds of both sexes are indistinguishable in the field; except for their faces, all resemble winter-plumaged males. The cheek patches on winter females and on first-year birds range from grayish-white to off-white. A suffused brown or black streak runs horizontally from the base of the lower mandible to the nape, which varies from brown to gray. On some first-year males, the dark, horizontal face streak may be faint or even lacking. Females in breeding plumage are often marked a rich reddish-brown on the breast, the flanks and in some cases, about the face.

In all plumages, both sexes have white underparts lightly barred brown or reddish-brown, white under-tail coverts, and black tail feathers. The

Top: Ruddy hens and first-year males are nearly distinguishable in appearance.
Bottom: Carvers who carve ruddys prefer the raised-tail drake as their subject.

Ruddy Duck Measurements				
	Adult Male	**Adult Female**	**Immature Male**	**Immature Female**
Length	14.7–16.0 in. Average 15.4 in.	14.5–16.2 in. Average 15.1 in.		
Wing	5.8 in.	5.5 in.	5.7 in.	5.6 in.
Weight	0.6–1.4 lbs. Average 1.2 lbs.	1.0–1.4 lbs. Average 1.19 lbs.	1.0–1.4 lbs. Average 1.18 lbs.	0.6–1.2 lbs. Average 0.76 lb.

underwings are grayish and the median under-wing coverts are white.

RANGE AND HABITAT

Along with the cinnamon teal, the ruddy duck is the only waterfowl to breed in both North and South America. Preferred nesting habitats include prairie sloughs and freshwater marshes, lakes, and ponds. In North America, the nominate race is a widespread breeder in the Prairie Provinces of Canada, the Pacific states, and the northwestern and north-central states south to New Mexico, Arizona, western Texas, and central Mexico. It breeds sporadically in the Northeast in a large area surrounding the two eastern-most Great Lakes. In South America, two additional races breed on Andean lakes from Columbia to Chile.

Ruddy ducks winter on large bodies of fresh water or on shallow brackish bays, usually near or within about 100 miles of all U.S. coastlines (except in New England). They are also found in winter in Baja California, New Mexico, Arizona, southern Texas, Mexico, and along the Mississippi River north to southern Illinois.

COURTSHIP AND NESTING

The male ruddy displays by stretching his short neck upward and tilting his head backward. He swims slowly in front of the female, bowing and nodding as he goes. (The hen is often hidden in the rushes.) Observing this behavior, A.C. Bent wrote, "He knows he is handsome as he glides smoothly along without a ripple, his saucy sprigtail . . . pointed forward until it nearly meets his upturned head."

When finally approached by the female, the drake puffs out his chest, jerks his head forward repeatedly and beats his broad bill against his breast, at times striking the water. With seemingly great effort and with his tail cocked so far forward that it nearly touches his head, the drake emits a

Top: The drake ruddy—or "sprig-tail"—has an almost cartoon-like appearance. *Bottom:* Hens are smaller than drakes. The winter hens and the first-year birds have an off-white or grayish cheek patch with a blackish-brown streak that runs horizontally from the lower mandible to the nape.

soft, clucking sound. Male ruddy ducks do most of their displaying on the breeding grounds; rarely is the display performed during migration. Thus, it is thought that the display serves as much to proclaim territory as it does to cement pair bonding.

Ruddy ducks build basket-like nests of marsh plants in dense stands of bulrushes, phragmites, and cattails, usually about eight inches above the water and firmly attached to live vegetation. The growing plants are often arched over the nest to conceal it. Ruddies sometimes recycle the nests of other waterfowl and occasionally build their own nests on floating logs, mats of vegetation, or atop muskrat houses. Ruddies may lay their eggs in the nests of grebes or other ducks.

Each of the six to ten creamy white eggs is relatively large for so small a duck. Unusually large clutches may

Top: The ruddy duck is a small bird, measuring 14 to 16 inches in length with a wingspan of 21 to 24 inches. *Bottom:* Apparently uncomfortable in the mud, the ruddy is most often found on the water.

weigh three pounds or more, while the average hen weighs only a pound! Incubation lasts 23 to 26 days. The young are able to fly about seven or eight weeks after hatching.

FEEDING

Ruddy ducks are expert divers that feed almost exclusively on the bottoms of fresh or brackish lakes and ponds. Three-fourths of their food is plant matter: pondweed, duckweed, wild celery, smartweeds, wild rye, wild rice, algae, sedges, and grasses make up the bulk of the vegetarian portion of their diet. (Stems, roots, bulbs, seeds, husks, leaves, and filaments are consumed.) The final fourth of their fare consists of midge larvae, caddis flies, diving beetles, snails, and a variety of small crustaceans.

ODDS AND ENDS

In *The Encyclopedia of North American Birds*, John K. Terres lists an incredible 70 other names for the ruddy duck. "Stiff-tail" is perhaps the best known nickname, but other names like "bullneck," "bumblebee duck," "cock-tail," "creek coot," "dip-tailed diver," "dumb-bird," "mud dipper," and "sleepyhead" give the careful reader additional insight into the lives of these handsome little ducks.

The "bumblebee duck's" rapid, jerky flight with its whirring wingbeats is almost always close to the water. Flight is achieved only after desperate pattering across the surface for some distance with its large feet; its small, rounded wings alone cannot get it airborne. Migration is thought to take place almost exclusively at night: have you ever seen a flock of ruddies on the wing?

Much of the literature states that except for keeping company with coots, ruddy ducks, or "creek coots," seldom associate with other duck species. At Jamaica Bay, however, it is not unusual to see a pair of lesser scaups or gadwalls feeding with a group of ruddies. In general,

The duck's broad bill serves the bottom feeder well when it seeks food in lakes and ponds. Most of their food is plant matter but they will also eat insects and small crustaceans.

Hens are much less striking than the drakes. However, both hens and drakes are white underneath, with lightly barred under-tail coverts and black tail feathers.

ruddy ducks are not very active and spend a great deal of time loafing and floating with their heads tucked into their back feathers, hence the name "sleepyhead."

Ruddy duck populations have been declining for many decades, in part due to their tameness—these "dumb-birds" are fairly easy to hunt. The drainage of wetlands and the occurrence of periodic droughts and floods have also had adverse effects on ruddy duck numbers.

In the 1950s, the ruddy duck was introduced into England and now populates parts of Europe where it inter-breeds with its close relative the white-headed duck. Ornithologists are greatly concerned with the fate of the native species. An international workshop held early in 1994 recommended that control measures be taken. In Europe, the ruddy is both a rogue and a villain.

In the Americas, though, the delightful little ruddy duck is a favorite of birders and carvers alike. A sky-blue-billed, chestnut-red drake floating amidst green shadows and rushes on a still May morning is one of nature's most beautiful sights.

Greater and Lesser Scaup
(*Aythya marila, Aythya affinis*)

BY RICK BURKMAN

Opening Pages: A lesser scaup drake comes in for a landing. The scaup, greater and lesser, is a popular subject for carvers, who often call these diving ducks "bluebills." *Above:* The greater scaup lacks the head bump of the lesser scaup. Greater scaup also have more iridescent green in the head coloring while the lesser has more purple.

E very year flocks of ducks, primarily greater and lesser scaup, fill the skies over the bays near my Lake Superior home. The wonder of migration is an exquisite mystery, but we know what it means—winter is on the way. Yet the cycle continues year to year and we wait expectantly for the day when the ducks arrive, even though we know that ice, snow, and cold will follow in their wake.

Scaup are one of the largest and most abundant of the big-water ducks. They come in two sizes: the larger is the greater scaup (*Aythya marila*) and the smaller is the lesser scaup (*Aythya affinis*). Because the two ducks are strikingly similar in appearance it's easy to confuse them in the field and, sometimes, even when holding them in the hand. The males of both species have dark heads, lightly colored bodies, and dark hind ends—think of a football-shaped Oreo® cookie. The females, on the other hand, are brownish-colored overall with some lighter head markings. Even expert birders can have trouble separating the two.

However, there are ways to tell them apart. The more cosmopolitan greater scaup frequents marine and brackish habitats in the world's northern parts, while the lesser scaup prefers seasonal wetlands, freshwater bays, and lakes with emergent vegetation on the North American continent. The greater scaup winters in the marine environments of the northeastern United States while the lesser scaup spends the cold season along the Atlantic seaboard, the Gulf of Mexico, most of Central America, and north to the northern boundary of Washington state. The greater scaup may live all around the northern globe, but it is the lesser scaup that knows where to find seasonal warmth.

Head shape provides the first visual clue to speciation. Greater scaup are round-headed and lesser scaup, which are marginally smaller, have squarer heads. Of course, things are never that simple. Lesser scaup do appear more square-headed, with feathering that creates a small bump or point at the rear crown, but under the right wind conditions or posture the greater scaup can also appear to have a small head bump. To make it even more confusing, lesser scaup can occasionally lower their bump so that they appear round-headed.

Male head color is equally important for both field identification and

A greater scaup drake turns its back on the photographer to reveal its tail structure and the arrangement of its primaries.

Greater Scaup Measurements				
	Adult Male	**Adult Female**	**Immature Male**	**Immature Female**
Length	16.5–20.2 in. Average 18.6 in.	15.5–18.7 in. Average 17.0 in.		
Wing		8.45 in.	8.64 in.	8.34 in.
Weight	1.9–3.0 lbs. Average 2.32 lbs.	1.6–2.8 lbs. Average 2.15 lbs.	1.8–2.5 lbs. Average 2.18 lbs.	1.8–2.6 lbs. Average 2.17 lbs.

Lesser Scaup Measurements				
	Adult Male	**Adult Female**	**Immature Male**	**Immature Female**
Length	15.8–17.9 in. Average 17.0 in.	15.2–17.5 in. Average 16.5 in.	15.8–17.9 in. Average 16.9 in.	15.2–17.5 in. Average 16.3 in.
Wing	8.2 in.	8.0 in.	8.1 in.	7.8 in.
Weight	1.1–2.4 lbs. Average 1.82 lbs.	1.0–2.1 lbs. Average 1.65 lbs.	1.1–2.1 lbs. Average 1.71 lbs.	1.0–2.1 lbs. Average 1.62 lbs.

carving, but even here the subtleties prove challenging. Both types of scaup have black heads, so observing the subtle iridescent sheen reflecting from their head feathers becomes important. The lesser scaup's head, under the right conditions, shows a purple or green iridescence; the greater scaup has a green iridescence—never purple.

Their broad blue bills (which provide the colloquial name for both species: bluebills) appear equally similar and require careful observation. The bill of the greater scaup is wider

Top: There's a reason people call these ducks bluebills. This is a lesser scaup. *Below:* The white in front of the bill is characteristic of the hen scaup, both lesser (pictured here) and greater. The greater scaup hens also have a light ear patch.

A lesser scaup drake shows off its wingspan and the vermiculation on its back. The white band on the bird's secondaries fades into a gray on the primaries.

and deeper and the nail on the tip is bigger than that of the lesser scaup. The bills are well designed, with straining lamella that the birds employ to grab prey in the water or root through lake-bottom mud to capture scuds (freshwater creatures that resemble small shrimp), midge larvae, leeches, mollusks, water bugs, and plant seeds.

FEEDING

Mollusks were recently discovered to be a highly prized food source for both the greater and lesser scaup. Their feeding habitats have changed in the last 50 years and scaup now like to feed around the water-intake valves of power plants even though few birds are strong enough to escape the currents these large structures generate. A 1993 count of the stomach contents of 21 lesser scaup killed by the water-intake structures at a nuclear power plant in Michigan revealed that 19 of the birds had large numbers of zebra mussels in their stomachs and proventricula. One bird had a whopping 987 of the little bivalves in its gullet!

Zebra mussels are an invasive species but as filter feeders they have no peer—and that creates a steep price for the scaup. As the ducks gorge on zebra mussels their bodies accumulate hazardous or even toxic contaminants from the mussels. Some researchers believe this is one of the main reasons why the lesser scaup population has decreased by 50 percent over the past 50 years.

Adult greater and lesser scaup feed almost exclusively below the surface. They arch their bodies and plunge into the depths, where they kick and swim as they sweep their bills through the mud and silt at the bottom of the lake, bay, estuary, or river. Lesser scaup can dive below the surface on the day they hatch, but they pop up quickly at this

young age. By five weeks of age they can stay underwater for 25 seconds. The ducks do not dive straight down and then pop back up. Instead, they dive at an angle and resurface up to 18 meters away—but only after searching the water bottom, chasing minnows, and nabbing any food tidbits that pass their way.

In the air scaup fly rapidly with fast wing beats. Observers on the ground can note some subtle wing markings to distinguish the two species. The best wing clue is the amount of white on the extended or flying wings. Greater scaup have a whitish color that extends to the inner six primary feathers. The lesser scaup has less white on the wings. It extends only across the secondaries, with the white fading to a gray that extends into the inner primaries. In my experience, the glare from water and sky, the speed of moving birds, and some crossover between the

Note the blockier and less-rounded shape of the lesser scaup's head. The bill lends itself to dredging lake and river bottoms.

Top: The greater scaup has a much more rounded head than the lesser scaup. *Above:* Vermiculation, whether it's on a scaup or some other duck, always provides carvers with a challenge during the painting process.

A greater scaup drake displays its flexibility as it preens mid-lake. The pose also offers an opportunity to observe the inside of the bill.

two ducks in wing coloration make accurate wing observation at a distance very challenging.

Determining differences between the species is difficult enough in the males—like many bird species, they appear to our eyes to be the more colorful, or at least colorfully contrasting, of the genders. The females, however, are so similar that sometimes it's almost impossible to make a definitive identification. The hen scaup of both types are brown birds with a white feather border at the base of the bill, but with few other distinctive field marks. Like the males, some differences in wing pattern and head shape can provide clues to the female's identification, and the greater scaup is slightly larger than the lesser scaup, but differences are subtle and confusing. The most easily visualized characteristic is the auricular, or ear, patch that many greater scaup females have. Unfortunately, there is noth-

ing easy about this duck—a few lesser scaup females can also have small, lightly colored auricular patches.

BREEDING

Identification challenges aside, the scaup apparently know the difference between greater and lesser. Both the greater and lesser will crossbreed with a variety of other deep water and puddle ducks, including American wigeon, canvasbacks, ferruginous ducks, redheads, ring-necked ducks, tufted ducks, and wood ducks. The results are strange hybrids that share the characteristics of both adults. Strangely, the greater and lesser scaup rarely interbreed with one another and hybrids between these two similar species are extremely rare.

Both have somewhat similar habits when it comes to nesting. After forming a pair bond the expectant parents fly around grasslands, open areas, and water edges searching for the ideal place to build a nest. The nest begins as a simple scrape in the ground that the female scaup will visit once per day to deposit a single egg. Each time she makes her daily visit the hen weaves a few nearby grasses into the nest bowl, adds a few downy feathers, and then leaves until the next day. After she has between 8 to 10 eggs in the nest she is ready to begin incubating the brood. Both greater and lesser scaup eggs are olive-colored, but the greater scaup's eggs are noticeably larger than those of the lesser scaup. Because many of these ducks nest in the far north, if the first nest fails they will rarely make an attempt at a second nest in a season.

A little more than three weeks will pass before the eggs start hatching. Within 24 hours all of the eggs have hatched and the brood has moved to a nearby wetland to feed and grow. In good breeding areas the ducks may form brood crèches where hundreds of ducklings of several ages will swim and feed together under the watchful eyes of six or more vigilant females. Within two weeks the ducklings are routinely diving underwater to obtain food, learning the skills that will last them a lifetime. After about 50 days the young are ready to fly and the family bonds begin dissolving. Males have moved on to larger bodies of water to finish molting and prepare for their long migration. Hens and young birds begin to form rafts, sometimes numbering in the thousands, as they prepare for their late fall journeys away from the cold to more hospitable climates.

Scientists still want to know more about these birds. Not only has their diet changed in the last 50 years, climate change may be altering their nesting and migration patterns as well. As is the case with many birds, much remains to be discovered and the future is unpredictable, but one thing remains the same—long flights over a watery horizon of hundreds of scaup is a sure sign that snowflakes and chill winds will soon arrive.

Surf Scoter
(*Melanitta perspicillata*)

BY RICK BURKMAN

Opening pages: There's no confusing the surf scoter with any other bird. The large and colorful bill gives it away every time. *Above:* The bill's bright orange, white, and black pattern with an orange tip marks this as an adult male.

The surf scoter (*Melanitta perspicillata*) has been accurately described as a velvety-black bird with a harlequin nose. The large bill, with its clown-like colors of red, orange, white, and black, is easily the most striking feature of this sea duck. Like many products of nature, the super-sized bill of the Surf scoter is more than a showpiece—it's a tool powerful enough to pull clams, oysters, and other hard-bodied creatures from underwater rocks, and to crack the hard shells of their prey to reach the succulent meat inside. The bill's unusual shape and size may bring to mind the time when people like W. C. Fields and, later, Jimmy Durante delighted the world by capitalizing on their oversized proboscis, but for the scoter it's a means of survival in the tumbling surf they call home.

Surf scoters are uniquely North American birds, breeding and wintering within this continental territory. Individual birds may make occasional forays to Siberia or other nearby landmasses, but it lives and breeds only in Alaska and across the northern reaches of Canada. They spend their winters swimming in the surf of both the Pacific and Atlantic coasts, from Alaska in the west to Quebec and New Brunswick in the east, then as far south as the Sea of Cortez along the coasts of Baja California, the Gulf of Mexico, and up the eastern seaboard.

They spend their days in flocks riding on the water, diving in unison like a flotilla in formation as they feed on hard-shelled invertebrates and fish eggs in the rich near-shore waters. They dive as a group then suddenly reappear, each bird breaking to the surface to eat their prey and breathe before diving to the depths of the cold waters again. Diving and resurfacing in unison may be a protection against gulls, which have been known to steal food from the bills of foraging scoters.

PAIR BONDING

Male surf scoters can outnumber females by as much as two to one, so competition is fierce for pair bonding, and there are more disappointed males than there are females. Pair bonding begins on the birds' wintering grounds. Drakes swim rapidly back and forth in front of the female, trying to get her attention. They dip their bill in the water and then tuck it into their breast to show its resplendent color against a backdrop of deep black feathers. He lifts his chin to the sky, twists his head from side to side, and then abruptly turns away from her so she can see his brightly erect white nape marking. The males make short, teasing flights away from and back to the female. He lands with a spray and a splash, neck erect and wings held straight up over his back—a proud display that shows his vibrancy and strength to its fullest extent.

After showing off his colors, strength, and overall vitality and vigor, the drake still does not know if he will be the chosen one; as many as six suitors may be vying for the attention of a single female. But, eventually, the

A scoter demonstrates that the bill isn't just for show—it's utilitarian. It's especially useful for pulling shellfish from their lairs and cracking the shells. Notice the white patch visible on the nape of the neck. The patch sometimes has an irregular fringe at the bottom.

Surf Scoter Measurements

	Adult Male	Adult Female	Immature Male	Immature Female
Length	18.0–20.9 in. Average 19.7 in.	17.0–19.0 in. Average 18.5 in.		
Wing	9.5 in.	8.9 in.	9.2 in.	8.9 in.
Weight	1.4–2.5 lbs. Average 2.2 lbs.	1.5–2.2 lbs. Average 2.0 lbs.		

duck dives underwater and the males quickly follow. Males pop to the surface, one-by-one, and the one that surfaces with the female is the newly chosen mate.

The pair remains together as they migrate north to their breeding lands in the boreal and taiga forests of Canada and Alaska. However, despite the time and effort involved in forming the pair bond, domestic coupling is short-lived. The male leaves the female within three weeks of arriving on her breeding lake. He joins large flocks of other males on large bodies of water,

Surf scoters, also known as "coots," breed in freshwater ponds across northern Canada but spend most of the year along both North American coasts. While the scoter is a popular subject for carvers, diners tend to avoid the strongly flavored bird.

Surf scoters often forage in the high-energy surf, where they dive through breaking waves to snatch their prey. A suitable habitat for a decorative sculpture might include waves and splashing water.

like Hudson Bay, to molt and fatten before beginning the fall migration.

However, the female does not waste time pining over her missing mate. Northern summers are brief and the serious work of raising a new generation of scoters cannot wait. A ground nest made of mosses, spruce or pine needles, and nearby grasses is quickly constructed under a fallen log or below a spray of overhanging branches. A few feathers create a layer of soft insulation for her precious charges. Once the nest is complete she begins laying her clutch of six to nine creamy white, smooth-shelled eggs. It is presumed that a new egg is added to the nest every one and one-half days, although direct evidence of the laying pattern is lacking.

Incubation is believed to be similar to that of a Barrow's goldeneye, lasting 28 to 30 days. All of the eggs hatch within a few hours of one another. The young emerge, downy feathers wet from the time spent trapped and growing within their shells. The downy feathers of the precocial ducklings quickly dry, and the brown and gray fluff balls are soon ready to follow their mother as they brave a strange new world.

RAISING DUCKS

Scoter ducklings are led to a nearby lake or pond where they begin foraging for themselves. They thrive on an abundant diet of invertebrates like beetles, dragonflies, leeches, mayflies, and nematodes. The bloom of invertebrates in the short summer season provides the young with a rich diet; they increase their weight an amazing 18-fold in only 55 days.

Small broods in heavy nesting areas inevitably meet. Ducklings can be swapped, and although females may chase strange youngsters, exchanges eventually occur, especially if the young are persistent. Broods with as many as 30 ducklings have been observed, likely the result of brood amalgamation.

While the ducklings are small, the mother valiantly protects her brood. She warns them of danger, shelters them under her wings during bad weather, and keeps them close at night. But there are dangers in a land where every living organism is part of the intricate web that makes up the food chain. Crows, ravens, gulls, foxes, and mink relish the eggs of ground-nesting birds and gladly dine on young birds if

they can catch them. Eagles snatch unsuspecting birds from the surface of the water, and even loons appear to be an important duckling predator. Scoter mothers quickly move their young toward the shoreline if loons are present, in the apparent hope that loons cannot travel in water that is too shallow. As the ducklings grow, the parental bond becomes weaker, and the mother usually abandons the brood before they begin to fly.

Although the target of many predators, the scoter does not appeal to the human palate. According to some writings from the 1600s, scoters could be eaten during the religious period of Lent. However, later authors questioned its palatability. Walter H. Rich in his 1902 book *Feathered Game of the Northeast* writes about the table fare of the scoters, or "coots," as they were once called: "They are unusually tough customers either in life or at the table. Most of our cooks believe it impossible to so prepare this bird as to make it decent food for any but a starving man. The best recipe I have seen runs somewhat as follows: First, skin your fowl and let it parboil in saleratus [baking soda, Ed.] water at least one day, or until it can be dented with a fairly sharp ax. If your courage holds out, the game is now ready to stuff and bake as you would any other duck, except that you must put enough onions into its inside to take away all coot flavor. Arriving at this stage of proceeding there are two lines of retreat yet open to you; either throw your delicate morsel away or give it to someone against whom you hold an ancient grudge—on no account should you try to eat it."

Obviously, Rich was not a fan of coot stew. But what surf scoters lack in flavor, they make up in beauty. Their velvety black bodies provide a colorful backdrop to the red, yellow, orange, and black bill. Their white eye and white nape patch create a

White-winged scoters aren't as flashy as the surf scoters—especially the juveniles pictured here. The adults are all black, or dark brown, with a flashy white speculum and a white swoosh under the eyes.

The coloring of the female surf scoter is much more subdued than the drake's. The vertical white patch in front of the eyes is one of its more prominent identifiers. Hens and drakes have short and sturdy wedge-shaped tails.

sharp contrast to their black bodies and create a nattily dressed sea duck.

Unfortunately, this sea duck with the bulbous nose has been scientifically neglected, possibly due to its remote habitat or lack of acceptance as table fare. Even now, much of the knowledge that biologists have is based on the behavior of related species, like the black scoter, white-winged scoter, and Barrow's goldeneye. Basic information on its breeding biology, reproductive success, and criteria for choosing wintering or breeding sites is unknown. Population estimates and causes of population changes are not well enough understood to provide criteria for successful management. Only now is it finally becoming the subject of study for avian researchers. Current research has revealed migration patterns, wintering preferences, travel routes, and more. With skill, and a little bit of luck, ornithologists and biologists will learn more about this duck, and that will benefit all who love the wilderness and the creatures that live there.

Northern Shoveler
(Anas clypeata)

BY STEVE MASLOWSKI

Opening pages: Look at the northern shoveler and your eyes are almost irresistibly drawn to the oversized bill that gives this duck its name. *Above:* Although the hen lacks the drake's colorful plumage, the bill remains just as eye-catching.

Every species in nature has its niche—its special role, place, and way of life. For some animals, such as the mallard, this niche encompasses a wide range of habitats and activities. The mallard needs a place to dabble, but beyond that, this jack-of-all-trades can make do with whatever the habitat happens to offer. The northern shoveler is different. Its peculiar oversized bill is almost a billboard proclaiming specialization. That bill affects the shoveler's life in many ways.

The origin of the shoveler's name seems to stem from the appearance of its bill. While the current name suggests it looks like a shovel, not long ago the shoveler's scientific name was *spatula clypeata* (since changed to *anas clypeata*). A still popular colloquial name is "spoonbill." To me, shoveler and spoonbill achieved popularity because they are easy to say and have a poetic sound—especially when compared to "shoehorn strainerbill," which might be a more appropriate moniker. The bill, which is twice as wide at the end as at the base, most resembles the gracefully curved and tapered metal gadget that helps us put on new shoes. In function, the shoveler's bill performs like a strainer. With these neat tools right by its mouth, the shoveler is all set to rustle up vittles.

DUCK OF THE MUCK

The right place to dine is the most important aspect of habitat for a shoveler. It needs lots of shallows rich with plant and animal life. Here it cruises slowly, using its bill to either skim the top or work slightly below the surface, sometimes partly submerging its head to get an optimum depth. The shoveler also at times simply stands in mud to forage. The bill works rapidly as it is swung from side to side and opened and closed in short little chops. Water and foods are sorted and strained all the while by comb-like structures, called lamellae, rimming the sides of both the upper and lower bill just inside the cutting edges.

The lamellae of the top and bottom bills mesh together and allow water to be expelled but retain solids. Pressure to force out the water is provided by the tongue, which is full of sensitive nerves for sorting out favorite food items from the general muck. For shovelers, the list of edibles from both the plant and animal kingdoms is quite lengthy. Their respective quantities depend upon the kind of soup the shoveler happens to be slurping—perhaps it is a green vegetable minestrone with lots of algae and seeds, or maybe it's a good hearty arthropod and mollusk stew.

Shovelers are taxonomically close to teal, and share the same kind of shallow water habitat. However, teal and other dabblers are fond of tipping and feeding off the bottom. The shoveler can tip, but rarely does. This difference allows the birds to congenially cohabit the same places. On a couple of occasions, I have seen shovelers kick teal off resting areas, so it seems that teals are the guests of shovelers rather than vice versa.

The shoveler's profile on the water is distinct. It seems as if the shoveler's oversized bill presents a heavy burden, because the bill invariably slants down, whereas most other ducks point theirs out straight and level with the water. Moreover, the entire front of the bird rides low in the water. The tilt, however, is probably not because of the bill's weight;

You could call the shoveler the original muckraker. The birds use their unique bills to sort and strain food from the mud. The birds tend to swim with the bill pointed down, while other ducks keep their bills level.

Northern Shoveler Measurements

	Adult Male	Adult Female	Immature Male	Immature Female
Length	19.0–20.2 in. Average 19.4 in.	18.0–20.0 in. Average 18.7 in.	18.5–19.5 in. Average 19.2 in.	17.1–18.5 in. Average 17.8 in.
Wing	9.6 in.	9.0 in.	9.3 in.	8.8 in.
Weight	1.1–1.8 lbs. Average 1.5 lbs.	1.1–1.7 lbs. Average 1.4 lbs.	1.0–1.8 lbs. Average 1.4 lbs.	0.7–1.6 lbs. Average 1.3 lbs.

Left, top and bottom: The hens are not as colorful as the drakes but their feathers have their own intricate patterns. The colors darken and become drabber during the mating and nesting period, helping the hen escape detection by predators. *Above:* Shovelers tend to congregate on mud flats and shallow shorelines, places where they can best put their bills to work.

the low angle improves the bird's ability to skim the water while feeding.

Shovelers favor areas with lots of shallow shorelines or mud flats where feeding is best. During nesting season, the shoveler haunts a wide swatch of prairie potholes and marshland from northern Kansas up to Alaska, where it follows the broad valley of the Yukon River. Across much of this area the shoveler abounds, occupying nearly every pond and flooded marsh large enough to raise a brood. If, during the course of summer, the pond gets stagnant or dries to the point where the shoveler is filtering as much mud as water, so much the better. This concentrates the food supply. To paraphrase J. C. Phillips, who wrote about shovelers and other ducks in the 1920s, filth is not essential for shovelers, but soft, slimy mud is what they seem to want. The species is also noted for tolerance of pollution, and regularly visits sewage and sediment ponds.

MIGRATION

The northern shoveler's nesting range includes parts of Europe and Asia, making the species one of the more widespread ducks on a worldwide basis. Three other shoveler

Above: The oversized bill seems to throw off the proportions of a shoveler in flight, making the wings seem set further back than they are on other ducks. *Left:* The green iridescence of the head feathers offers a painting challenge and the bird's overall variety of colors and feather patterns make it a worthy subject for carving.

they like to feed. During migration shovelers can be seen in almost any of the lower 48 states, in part because some migrate diagonally across eastern states to reach the warm southeastern corner of our continent. By mid-November, most shovelers have reached winter destinations, though a few rugged birds may linger north until hard winter sets in. Principle wintering grounds have virtually no overlap with the nesting grounds. Large numbers of shovelers haunt inland and brackish waters of the west coast from Oregon south through most of Mexico. Shovelers also rim

species in the southern hemisphere give the clan an even more cosmopolitan flair.

Despite a nesting season that starts rather late, the shoveler migrates early in fall, joining teal and woodies in southward flight beginning about mid-September. Shovelers seem to avoid ice, which typically forms first in the shallow shoreline waters where

Male shovelers in their nuptial plumage have a gray-blue shoulder patch separated from a brilliant green speculum by a tapered white stripe. The tertials are long, pointed, and black, with a white midrib.

the Gulf of Mexico and vacation across Florida and the Caribbean.

Usually wintering birds are seen only a few at a time, perhaps mingling with teal, pintail, or other dabblers. Flocks of 25 to 50 occur frequently, but only on rare occasions where there is an exceptional food source are shovelers apt to gather by the thousands like mallards or scaup.

In the course of migration, shovelers generally do not have to dodge the thicket of flying steel shot awaiting more popular species of waterfowl. Even though shovelers settle naively into decoys, they just are not a duck of choice for most hunters, and may be passed over if there are pintails or mallards in the area. The shoveler's omnivorous diet, liberally laced with insects, crustaceans, and other forms of aquatic animal life, often yields a duck with an unappealing fishy flavor.

When the shoveler flies, its oversized bill makes the shoveler's wings seem to be set back on the body a little farther than for most ducks. The shoveler's flight can be erratic like a teal's, though it is a little slower. Shovelers leap straight up off the water when flushed.

Probably because the shoveler has never been a prime target for sportsmen and is not especially common in the great waterfowling/carving areas of the east, the shoveler was largely absent from display shelves. In two of my favorite decoy reference books, I could not find a single example of a shoveler. Perhaps, too, there were more subtle reasons for the shoveler's omission in decoys, especially decorative ones. A bird that spends its life filtering slimy ooze doesn't create a wild, romantic cachet for itself. Also, despite the fact that the plumage of the drake is very striking, the shoveler's big beak dominates its appearance. That bill stands out like the painted oversized smile of a clown. In fact, a common local name for the bird in some areas is "grinner," as in grinning mallard. The shoveler does not have the elegance of canvasbacks, black ducks, and pintails.

Nevertheless, carvers have been reconsidering shovelers in recent years. Shovelers offer potential for wonderful, fresh, innovative work. And the adult male wears a striking plumage, which is outclassed by only a handful of other ducks. From stem to stem the shoveler is a bird you cannot help but notice.

Black-bellied and Fulvous Whistling–Ducks
(Dendrocygna autumnalis, Dendrocygna bicolor)

BY RICK BURKMAN

Opening pages: Back off! A black-bellied whistling-duck strikes a threatening pose. *Above:* Unlike other ducks, black-bellied whistling-ducks mate for life.

Whistling-ducks, once known as tree ducks, are one of the oddities of the waterfowl world. Although they are called ducks, their unusually upright posture is more reminiscent of the goose or swan family than of the duck clan. Even their scientific genus name *Dendrocygna* translates as "tree swan," suggesting a kinship to these larger waterfowl.

These are not the only similarities whistling-ducks have with geese and swans. The male and the female whistling-ducks look alike, as do male and female geese and swans; they generally bond to their mates for life; their bonding rituals are not elongated, elaborate, or showy like most other ducks; and the males help raise the young birds after hatching.

Whistling-ducks do not quack and grunt like many other ducks—instead they have a loud, piercing call, not quite a whistle, as their name implies. The black-bellied whistling-duck's call sounds like a group of squabbling shorebirds, and the fulvous whistling-ducks's call is a two-part squeal that sounds vaguely like a jay or small hawk.

Whistling-ducks do not have a wide distribution on the North American continent, being restricted primarily to the southern coastal regions and areas of the Southwest. However, they are one of the world's most common duck groups and are found in the tropical and subtropical marshes and wetlands around the world.

BLACK-BELLIED WHISTLING-DUCK

The black-bellied whistling-duck is the only North American whistling-duck that will occasionally perch in trees to rest, preen, and view its surroundings. Black-bellied whistling-ducks flap their way through tree groves in portions of southern California, Arizona, Texas, Louisiana, and Florida. These southernmost parts of the United States are actually the northern reaches of the duck's home range—the majority of the population is found in the marshes and waterways of Central and South America.

Black-bellied whistling-ducks, like their distant cousins, the wood ducks, hooded mergansers, and some of the other northern tree-nesting ducks, will occasionally alight in trees, but they often have ulterior motives—they are searching for trees with hollowed areas caused by disease, age, or woodpeckers and other animals that leave openings suitable for use as nest cavities. The parents-to-be land in tree branches above these potential nesting sites, and they will arch their necks and twist their heads to peer into the depths of the cavities below them.

Little work is done to complete the nest once a cavity is chosen. The ducks may enter the nest cavity, wiggle around for comfort, and, with that, the nest is complete. With the exception of the feathers that fall off during the egg-laying and incubation period and the rotted wood chips and normal detritus found at the bottom of tree cavities, there is no lining added to cushion or protect the eggs.

When nest cavities are not readily available, the black-bellied whistling-duck will nest on the ground, creating a shallow scrape or depression below a thick clump of vegetation (sometimes including cacti), which gives a cavity-like feel.

Once the chosen cavity becomes a nest the female will lay between 9 and 18 white eggs. However, the actual number of eggs in a nest can vary greatly. Egg-dumping is common, and other whistling-ducks will lay their eggs in an occupied nest when the brood parents leave to feed or rest, resulting in layer upon layer of eggs in a single cavity. One nest reportedly had an astounding 101 eggs laid in it. The reason for egg-dumping, also known as brood parasitism, is un-

Admittedly not the most attractive duck species, the black-bellied whistling-duck looks and acts more like a member of the goose family.

Black-bellied Whistling-Duck Measurements		
	Adult Male	**Adult Female**
Length	18.7–19.8 in. Average 19.4 in.	18.5–20.0 in. Average 19.1 in.
Wing	9.2–9.8 in. Average 9.4 in.	9.0–9.7 in. Average 9.3 in.
Weight	1.50–2.00 lbs. Average 1.80 lbs.	1.44–2.25 lbs. Average 1.85 lbs.

Fulvous Whistling-Duck Measurements		
	Adult Male	**Adult Female**
Length	17.7–18.5 in. Average 18.1 in.	16.0–18.3 in. Average 17.3 in.
Wing	7.9–9.3 (all ducks)	
Weight	1.1–1.9 lbs. Average 1.72 lbs.	1.2–1.9 lbs. Average 1.49 lbs.

The adult black-bellied whistling-duck has a bright red bill, gray cheeks, a gray head with a brown cap, and a chestnut-colored chest. Although a water bird, it is known to perch in trees.

known, and the majority of eggs from such a large clutch will not survive.

After 26 days the young birds begin to get restless while still in their shells. They wiggle and call from inside their eggs, and on the 28th day of incubation each young bird will use the tiny egg tooth that has grown on the top of its bill to push and prod at the inside of the confining shell until a crack forms. Then it probes and pushes at the crack until, finally, it can force its wet, bedraggled head through the opening. After a moment's rest the birds continue to wiggle and squirm until they kick their bodies free—they are wet and tired, but ready to begin life's journey.

The young hatchlings quickly dry and turn into little balls of bright yellow and black fluff. They climb to their nest-hole entrance and dive into the world below. Their light weight, combined with their protecting layer of fluff, slows their descent and cushions their landing, making their entrance to the world a little less traumatic than it is for heavier creatures.

The ducklings quickly take to the water, following their parents in single file with the mother in the lead and father in the rear, in a pattern similar to goose families. If the young escape the world of predators—gulls from above, turtles, bass, and catfish from below—they will grow into handsome adult birds with bright red bills, large pink feet and legs, gray cheeks, gray heads with a brown cap, and chestnut-colored chests. One of their most striking colors, and the reason for their name, is their deep black abdominal feathers—the black belly of the black-bellied whistling-duck.

FULVOUS WHISTLING-DUCK

The fulvous whistling-duck is the nocturnal, globe-trotting cousin of the black-bellied whistling-duck. There are substantially similar resident populations of fulvous whistling-ducks found in Africa, Asia, Madagascar, North America, and South America, making this cosmopolitan bird an abundant and common wetland species. For genetically similar populations to occur around the world, the duck must have either migrated to these far-off regions or been blown by the force of large, moving storm systems to new lands. Despite its old name "tree duck," the fulvous duck does not actually perch in trees like the black-bellied duck does. Like many of its waterfowl cousins, it prefers to roost on the water or rest on nearby shorelines. And although these ducks prefer shallow wetlands, they have been sighted swimming on the deep waters of the Atlantic Ocean more than 1,200 miles from the nearest shore.

The adult fulvous whistling-duck has a tawny-brown belly and chest and blue-gray feet and bill. Like its black-bellied cousin, the fulvous shares many traits with members of the goose family.

Like geese, the hen and drake black-bellied whistling-ducks are similar in size. They stand upright like geese, too. The dark abdominal feathers are what give this duck its name. *Above:* While the black-bellied whistling duck reaches the southernmost portions of the United States, it mostly lives in the marshes and waterways of Central and South America.

At home the fulvous whistling-duck is a nocturnal feeder that travels nightly to its preferred feeding grounds. Shallow ponds, wetlands, and agricultural fields provide good sources of grains and weed seeds to satiate their appetites. However, to the chagrin of many farmers, these ducks have a particular fondness for cultivated rice fields. Although large numbers may cause localized damage to rice and agricultural fields, they also benefit wetland grain-growers by eating substantial amounts of weed seeds. When the early morning sun begins to rise they once again travel to their roosting areas to relax and while away the daytime hours resting, preening, and attending to the daily chores of body and feather maintenance.

Like the black-bellied whistling-duck, the fulvous whistling-duck appears more goose-like than duck-like. It stands upright, the male and female are similar in appearance and size; it mates for life; and the male and female share the incubation and brood-raising duties.

Unlike the black-bellied whistling-duck, the fulvous whistler does not nest in trees, although there have been in-

A black-bellied whistling duck offers its back to the camera. Notice how the brown crown continues down the back of the neck and how the pink legs and feet match the bill.

stances of these birds nesting in abandoned heron and eagle nests. The fulvous duck prefers to nest on the ground or on floating mats in areas of dense emergent vegetation. Nearby leaves, stems, and other plant materials are woven into the nest, but little additional cushioning, other than the feathers that fall from the birds as they enter or exit the nest area, is used. Part of the dense vegetation cover is pulled over the nest to conceal the spot, presumably from overhead predators.

After the nest is built the female fulvous duck begins laying eggs. Thirteen is the average number; however, the actual number laid is difficult to determine because, as with black-bellied whistling-ducks, egg-dumping is a common practice. The eggs are white- or buffy-colored ovals that quickly become stained by the color of the nesting materials and the organic-colored water that drips from the adults' wet bellies. The adults incubate the eggs for about 25 days, exchanging places every day or so to allow each one an opportunity to rest and feed away from the nesting area.

The ducklings will hatch within hours of one another and, after regaining the strength expended during their arduous struggle, they will leave the nest, protected by both parents. They swim, single-file, between the protecting adults as they explore their world. Young birds eat seeds, like their parents, but supplement their vegetable-based diet with insects and other invertebrates as they instinctively glean and scoop specks from the water's surface.

In 50 to 60 days the young birds look like grayer versions of the adults. In time, they will molt into their adult attire, with tawny-brown bellies and chests, blue-gray feet and bills, brown wings and backs, and a silvery border that separates the belly from the wings.

The whistling-ducks are expanding their range in North America. At one time the whistling-ducks were

Although the fulvous whistling-duck prefers shallow wetlands, people have spotted them swimming in the Atlantic Ocean more than 1,200 miles from land.

considered strictly a south-of-the-border species, living and thriving in Mexico and other areas of Central and South America. As they expand their range into the southern United States, more and more people will become familiar with these unique and beautiful additions to the world of waterfowl. And, with care, they will continue to thrill the world with their unique, goose-like waddle and unusual, un-duck-like whistling.

American Wigeon
(*Anus americana*)

BY STEVE MASLOWSKI

There may be confusion over what to call this species of duck—wigeon, widgeon, or baldpate—but most waterfowl enthusiasts are at least passingly familiar with it. *Anus americana* is common, widespread, and, in the case of the male, easy to identify.

One glance at the drake with his shining white crown and the origin of the moniker "baldpate" becomes obvious. Wigeon, however, is the term presently favored by the American Ornithologist Union, the governing body of bird names. The origin of the word wigeon is not entirely clear, but some linguistic authorities trace it back to an old French word for fool.

Living up to the meaning of its name, wigeons readily decoy to rigs of almost any species the hunter puts out. However, wigeons are not total fools, and after encoun-

Opening pages: In this shot of an American wigeon pair, the drake makes it readily apparent why this duck is also known as the "baldpate." *Top:* A wigeon in flight presents a fine study of its wing structure and coloring. The white shoulder patch is obvious. Wingspan is just under three feet. *Left:* The white outlines of the secondaries are easily seen in this rear view.

tering heavy hunting, they become quite wary.

Many people make their first acquaintance with wigeons far away from the duck blind. The birds often winter in city parks, where they lose much of their fear of man. At times they'll go shoulder to shoulder with mallards in pursuit of corn and bread tossed by children. It is interesting, though, to note that according to the late Al Hochbaum, a leading authority on ducks for the Delta Waterfowl Research Station, wigeons have a "heritable" wildness. That is, they simply cannot be domesticated like a mallard.

A DEVOUT VEGETARIAN

From breeding grounds in interior Alaska and the northern pothole prairie country of western provinces and states, wigeons migrate to our coastlines, the Deep South, and into Mexico and Central America. In a few select places, especially in California and Mexico, the wigeon can be the predominate wintering duck. But more often, it ranks at best a distant second or even lower behind mallards, pintails, or other locally abundant species. Overall, in most flyways, the wigeon seems to rank between third and fifth in abundance.

Hunters may not always actively pursue wigeons, but they'll rarely pass up a shot at the species. The wigeon's flavor ranks right up there with the best. Their quality is also dependable. At least 90 percent of the wigeon's

Wigeons, devoted vegetarians, will graze in fields like geese. In this view you can see how the breast feathers blend from brown to white at around the waterline. On average the wigeon weighs 1¼ pounds.

American Wigeon Measurements				
	Adult Male	**Adult Female**	**Immature Male**	**Immature Female**
Length	18.4–23.0 in. Average 20.3 in.	17.7–20.3 in. Average 19.0 in.	16.8–21.2 in. Average 18.6 in.	16.8–18.5 in. Average 17.3 in.
Wing	10.4 in.	9.7 in.	10.1 in.	9.6 in.
Weight	1.3–2.4 lbs. Average 1.81 lbs.	1.2–2.3 lbs. Average 1.69 lbs.	0.7–2.5 lbs. Average 1.75 lbs.	0.9–2.1 lbs. Average 1.56 lbs.

diet comes from the plant world. Thus, while mallards and pintails may from time to time supplement their diets with fish, crustaceans, and other animal matter, the wigeon remains as devout a vegetarian as the most honorable Chesapeake Bay canvasback. In fact, the wigeon's devotion to plant food is so strong that the species is known to resort to dishonorable means of obtaining it. Classified as a puddle duck, the wigeon has little skill at diving. In areas of deep water, it waits for true divers such as the canvasback to bring up morsels, then pilfers them.

Wigeons frequent marshes and fields, and sometimes haunt open lakes and bays with the divers. In the marshes it picks about like a coot, and in the fields it grazes around like a goose. The wigeon ranks as one of the most terrestrial of its genus (*Anus*), which includes mallards, pintails, gadwalls, and the like. In general, a wigeon's primary habitat consideration is reasonable access to its beloved, succulent plants.

QUIET, GENTLE, AND STUBBY

Wigeons fall in the medium range in terms of weight, wingspan, and other dimensions. A typical male is about 20–21 inches long, flies on a wingspan just under three feet (roughly 35 inches), and weighs $1^3/4$ pounds. By comparison, his mallard counterpart might weigh $2^1/2$ to 3 pounds.

Looking closely at the drake from stem to stem, the nail and tip of the bill are black, as may be the base and nostrils; but the bill is otherwise very

Wigeons have short, stubby bills, making them seem smaller than they really are. The nail and tip are black but the rest of the bill is a pale blue. The green eye band is one of the duck's striking trademarks. When on the water, the white shoulder patch just peeks out from beneath the scapular and side feathers.

From the front the wigeon's "baldpate" becomes much more obvious than it is in a side view. The head and neck provide a complex combination of colors and patterns.

The wigeon's upper body and back have a beautiful pattern of vermiculation. Carvers have developed various techniques to capture this look in their work. The primaries are dark gray and the secondaries are black outlined with white.

pale blue, as if washed with watercolor. The white crown begins at the bill and continues up and over the crown, then tapers to a point or fades away as it approaches the nape. From just forward of the eye, a green iridescent band swoops back toward the nape with a graceful curve and gives the impression of a broad racing stripe. This green can often dominate the back of the head, which otherwise tends to be heavily peppered black. The cheeks and neck are white or light tan, and randomly spotted and/or barred with black.

The upper body is a buffy gray finely vermiculated with black. At about the waterline of this high-riding duck the body color quickly shades to white. Beginning at roughly the end of the wing coverts the white goes up the rump in patch-like form, extending under the primaries. The end of the rump is black. The tail is also black with a white outline.

The wing coverts have the same color as the body and sometimes appear a darker gray. The primaries are dark gray. The secondaries protrude conspicuously. Four of them on each wing are long, black, and outlined with white. A white streak may also be evident in the forewing area of swimming or resting drakes. This forewing patch becomes very apparent in flying birds, and serves as one of the important field identification marks for hunters. The speculum features the same iridescent green as the eye stripe. From underneath, white shows prominently in the wing. The legs have the same pale robin-egg blue wash as the bill.

The hen wigeon presents greater problems for field identification. She closely resembles female gadwalls and pintails. The wigeon, however, has the white forewing, a blue bill, and a distinct contrast between the head and body. The upper half of her head—corresponding to the area of the white pate and green eyes in the male—tends to be darkly peppered, while the cheeks and neck have distinctly lighter specking. Her mantle is mottled in the same vein as hens of many species, with feathers that are dark interiorly and edged with buff.

Above: As in the male, the peppered patterns of the hen wigeon's head end quite abruptly at the neck. The cheeks and neck have lighter specking. *Right:* A drake will form a pair-bond with a hen during the spring after migrating to more northern regions. The male will leave during the first week of incubation.

The overall impression a wigeon seems to give is one of being compact, quite rounded, and maybe a little stubby—perhaps because of its short bill. The wigeon also gives the impression of being a quiet, gentle duck. It doesn't seem to have the personality and flare of mallards, pintails, or other class leaders. But that is not at all to say the wigeon should be ignored. It has beautiful distinctive feathering, challenging lines, and a great deal of appeal in its own gentle way.

Wood Duck

(Aix sponsa)

BY FRANK C. BELLROSE

Opening pages: Long a favorite subject for wildfowl carvers, the drake wood duck displays a spectacular range of colors and patterns. While less flashy, the hen has her own charms. *Above:* A side view of the drake emphasizes many of its characteristics very well, including the crest, the bronze side feathers edged with black-and-white bars, the overlap of the wing by the side feathers, and the large tail that protrudes slightly upward.

Unique in many ways, the wood duck is an unusual species of waterfowl. It breeds more extensively and is confined within the borders of the continental United States more than any other duck. It is one of only six species of ducks that nest in tree cavities. The wood duck also commonly nests in towns and cities more than any other waterfowl, often utilizing cavities and nest houses in yards to become part of the urban wildlife scene. When the ducklings are about twenty-four hours old, they jump from their nests, often high in trees, at their mother's call, and follow her through forest and field, yards and factory to a preselected water area. This first trek may cover a mile or more!

Although wood ducks can tolerate man, they thrive in the wilderness. Canoeists meet the female and her brood of young on pristine streams. But adults and broods may be found almost anywhere that deciduous trees and shrubs, preferably overhanging, provide shoreline cover for some kind of water: streams, ditches, swamps, marshes, beaver ponds, and lakes. The wood duck's most important criteria in choosing a site are a place to nest, an adequate food supply, and cover, particularly for broods, in the nesting area.

About the only regions devoid of wood ducks are the most arid parts of the West and the Rocky Mountains. In Montana, a scattering of wood ducks breeds across the state along the Missouri, Yellowstone, and Bitterroot rivers.

Today, it is difficult to realize that at one time the wood duck was almost extinct. In the early 1900s, a number of eminent ornithologists predicted the demise of this species. Until the passage of the Migratory Bird Treaty Act of 1918 in conjunction with Canada, market-hunting of wood ducks was extensive, with open seasons from September to April. Because wood ducks, more than any other species, spent much of the year exposed to prolonged and intensive hunting, they benefited most from the new federal regulations; the season was closed to the killing of "woodies" until 1941, when the season was cautiously reopened with restrictions on the number that could be taken.

Although certain restrictions in the taking of wood ducks are still in effect, the bag has climbed steadily over the past three decades. Wood ducks are second in kill only to the ubiquitous mallard throughout the United States. Most wood ducks are taken east of the Great Plains.

Woodies are not great shakes as migrants, for they seldom fly more than a few hundred miles to reach their winter grounds. However, those that breed in northern Maine or Minnesota may migrate as far as 1,500 miles to find a hospitable southern swamp. Most of the wood ducks south of the

The head of the drake wood duck is the most brilliant of all waterfowl. The eye, 11 to 13 millimeters in diameter, is the largest among similarly sized ducks. Notice how the red iris and bill contrast with the multi-shaded greens and purples of the head.

Wood Duck Measurements				
	Adult Male	**Adult Female**	**Immature Male**	**Immature Female**
Length	18.8–21.2 in. Average 20.0 in.	18.5–20.1 in. Average 19.5 in.	15.9–18.5 in. Average 17.4 in.	15.1–17.8 in. Average 16.5 in.
Wing	8.9 in.	8.6 in.	8.6 in.	8.4 in.
Weight	1.2–1.9 lbs. Average 1.50 lbs.	1.1–1.9 lbs. Average 1.48 lbs.	1.1–1.8 lbs. Average 1.47 lbs.	1.0–1.8 lbs. Average 1.35 lbs.

The wood duck is one of the few duck species that nest in trees. Average clutch size is 12 eggs. When the chicks are only about a day old they make an incredible leap of faith, plunging from their tree-cavity nests to the ground at their mother's urging.

Mason-Dixon Line make local and area flights, but generally remain within the region throughout the year.

Shortly after the ice retreats from streams and lakes, the first pairs of wood ducks appear. These are adults, particularly the females, that are impelled northward by a physiological drive to return to their former nesting area. Other adult pairs and yearlings will follow during the next month. Depending upon the spring thaw, there may be a gap of several weeks between the arrival of birds on marginal wintering-breeding places and those arriving on far northern areas.

The adult female displays an amazing ability to locate and return to her former nest site. More often than not it is the same cavity or nest house that she used the preceding year. Yearling females also return to their natal areas but not to specific sites like their mothers. Adult females that were unsuccessful nesters and those that lost their nest sites to wind or occupancy of other animals join the yearlings in search of suitable sites.

Wood ducks usually search for nest sites in the first hour or two after daybreak, but occasionally search late in the afternoon. The pair flies to riparian timber, overflow-bottomland hardwoods, upland woods, and even wooded yards to check trees for cavities. From a horizontal limb high in the canopy, the female stretches and cranes her neck until she sees a hole. Flying to it she carefully peers in and, if it looks suitable and inviting, enters. She exits in a few moments and the pair flies to another tree or returns to its water area. I have watched a female inspect numerous cavities before selecting one.

The decayed wood or other debris in the base of a cavity or the sawdust in nest houses is rounded out by the female preparatory to the start of laying. Usually one egg per day is laid until a clutch of 12 is produced. However, clutches may vary from six to 40 or more eggs. A clutch of over 15 eggs indicates that more than one female has deposited eggs in the same day in the same nest house. Biologists term such situations as dump-nests, or compound clutches.

The first eggs laid are covered with the material forming the base of the nest. By the sixth egg, the female has placed a few down feathers plucked from her breast. Small amounts of down are added daily until the clutch is almost complete; then large amounts of down are added. The male accompanies his mate to the nest site each morning and stands guard while the egg is being deposited. This process may take from one-half to two hours.

Only the female incubates the eggs. Incubation usually takes 30 days but may vary from 28 to 37 days, depending upon the prolonged temperature the eggs receive. Incubating birds usually take a break of an hour or so each morning and late afternoon. Early in the incubation, the male follows his mate back to the nest site, but as incubation progresses, more drakes

The drake wood duck's markings are livelier than his female counterpart's. Note the abbreviated crest and the tan breast flecked with gray. The white, tear-shaped patch that goes to the back of the eye varies in size and is usually smaller in young hens during their first autumn.

desert their mates. Few drakes return up to the last day of incubation.

Unfortunately for the wood duck, nest destruction is 50 percent or higher in natural cavities. Nest houses built and positioned to inhibit the entry of certain predators have a higher nest success. Raccoons, squirrels, snakes, flickers, and starlings all pose varying threats to nesting woodies. The rac-

Wood ducks ride higher and more buoyantly when swimming than other ducks, as evidenced by the way the drake's tail rides an inch or so above the water's surface. When they leave the water the jet-propelled take-off requires only a few seconds.

coon prefers to capture the female on the nest and takes the eggs only if the bird escapes. Squirrels, bull and rat snakes, and flickers all destroy eggs to eat their contents. Starlings may be so aggressive in seeking a nest site that they drive incubating hens from their nests, resulting in desertion of the clutch.

A hen woodie that has escaped the vicissitudes of incubation to hatch a brood may spend another 60 to 70 days guarding her brood from predators and escorting them to food sources until they reach flight stage. Some females, especially those whose eggs hatched late, desert their young in their later growth stages. Of the 11 ducklings that leave the average successful nest, scarcely five survive to flight independence.

At hatching, a duckling weighs one ounce and in a few hours becomes a ball of fluffy down, almost black above,

sulphur-yellow below, with a dark stripe extending back from the eye. The first body feathers that form the juvenile plumage protrude through the down on the shoulder and tail at one week of age. Juvenile body feathers appear on the belly, breast, flank, head, neck, and back, in that order. By the time the young can fly, they are in full juvenile plumage; the male is showing red at the base of the bill and in the iris of the eye. Juvenile males now weigh 1.0–1.25 pounds, almost as much as adults. It will be another two months before the juveniles change to adult (nuptial) plumage.

Traditionally the wood duck is a denizen of swamps and overflow-bottomland hardwoods. This habitat preference is particularly evident in winter when southern rivers flood broad, flat bottomlands that have an abundance of oak, pecan, and hickories. Wood ducks quickly concentrate where acorns and other mast have accumu-

Traditionally, wood ducks are swamp dwellers. They tend to concentrate where they can find acorns, their favorite food. Notice the drake's crest, one of its most compelling features.

Facing page: The drake's burgundy breast has varying amounts of the white flecking; some birds have more and not in such ordered rows as the one shown here. *Top:* This rear view shows the side feathers overlapping the lower part of the wing with the long flight feathers (the primaries) protruding, their tips crossed. *Right:* Wood ducks habitually perch on logs, stumps, and floating debris, especially where woody cover overhangs the rest site.

lated in shallow water. When available, acorns are a favorite food, but otherwise the seeds of bald cypress, buttonbush, arrow arum, bur reed, and corn and other grains are utilized.

The crest, complex pattern, and shades of color of the male's plumage pose a real challenge to the duck carver and artist. In the duck decoy and art shows that I have judged, the wood duck has been the species in which I detected the most mistakes. Points that need to be carefully studied are its variety of colors (many of which change hue as the angle of light changes), the bronze side feathers edged with black and white, the multicolored crested head, the red-mar-

gined bill, the large red iris of the eye, and the large tail. The wood duck and the wigeon have the largest tails among game ducks (other than the long pointed tail of the pintail). Both have wedge-shaped tails, but the wood duck's is more square.

Woodcarvers and artists play an important role in waterfowl conser-

vation. By depicting the beauty of wood ducks and other waterfowl, they promote a greater interest among the public in the welfare of these birds. Because of wildlife photographers, artists, and carvers, there is an increasing awareness among hunters that there is more to a duck than meat on the table.

Brant

(Branta bernicla nigricans and Branta bernicla bernicla)

BY GARY KRAMER

Opening pages: One of the smallest goose species, brant enjoy dining on eelgrass. Carvers sometimes portray their brant with a bit of faux eelgrass dangling from the bill. *Above:* Atlantic brant breed farther north than most other waterfowl. You can find them in Canada's high arctic from Prince Patrick Island in the west to Southampton Island in the south, and east to the coast of Greenland.

Each autumn for centuries, black brant have migrated from their breeding grounds in Alaska to winter on the coastal bays and estuaries along the Pacific Coast. Likewise, a similar migration takes place by Atlantic brant from the high arctic of Canada and the coast of Greenland to wintering grounds along the Eastern Seaboard.

For as long as I can remember, I have been intrigued by waterfowl and their migrations. As a result of that interest, I spent two winters in the late 1970s in Mexico conducting graduate research on the winter ecology and migration patterns of Pacific brant.

One of my first duties was to conduct a census of the brant by counting those on the San Quintin Bay on the west coast of the Baja Peninsula (about 190 miles south of

San Diego). On November 7, 1974, I counted 275 brant at San Quintin. The next day, I made another count, and, to my astonishment, 8,000 birds were present!

Later that day, a telegram arrived from Alaska. In part, it read: "Brant exodus of major proportions from Izembek, 1600 to 2000 hours, November 5—be on the lookout for birds." My count took place the morning of November 8, and the migration time of brant between Izembek Lagoon, Alaska, and San Quintin Bay, Baja, California, was documented for the first time in history.

Since those early days, other biologists have studied brant migration and the flight time between Alaska and Mexico. The data shows that my first assessment of brant migration back in the 1970s still holds true today: the mi-

The neck of the brant is longer and more flexible than it might appear at times. When the brant is swimming its foreparts are black all the way to the waterline.

gration non-stop over a distance of 3,000 miles takes place in an average of 60 hours. That makes the average flight speed of the Pacific brant an amazing 50 miles per hour!

IDENTIFICATION AND HABITAT

There are three races, or subspecies, of brant worldwide: the Pacific, or black, brant (*Branta bernicla nigricans*), found along the west coast of North America; the Atlantic, or light-bellied, brant (*Branta bernicla hrota*), found on the east coast of North America; and the dark-bellied brant, or brent goose (*Branta bernicla bernicla*), which breeds in Siberia and winters in Europe.

The most notable field identification marks are the small patch of white on the upper neck and the striking white ventral region on the otherwise dark body. All three subspecies are similar in appearance and size. Brant are among the smallest of the geese, averaging just over three pounds. The most notable difference between the North American races is that the underparts of the Atlantic race are much lighter than those of the Pacific.

Brant spend their lives near saltwater, nesting in coastal tundra and wintering on bays, lagoons, and estuaries. Their diet on the breeding grounds is comprised of sedges and rushes, while in winter they rely heavily on eelgrass, a submerged aquatic plant that grows in tidal areas.

In the 1930s, a disease wiped out the eelgrass beds on the Atlantic coast and many brant, unable to adapt to other foods, perished. Other brant changed their food habits to include sea lettuce, wigeon grass, and salt-marsh grasses. Today, sea lettuce and

Pacific (Black) Brant Measurements		
	Adult Male	**Adult Female**
Length	24–26 in. Average 25 in.	22–25 in. Average 23 in.
Wing	12.1 in.	11.6 in.
Weight	3.19 lbs.	2.88 lbs.

The most notable difference between the North American varieties of brant is that the underparts of the Atlantic brant are much lighter than those of the Pacific version.

eelgrass are the primary winter foods of Atlantic brant. Similar eelgrass diseases and a subsequent change in food habits have not occurred on the west coast.

BREEDING

Brant form pair bonds on the wintering grounds, and, once mated, are monogamous until one of the individuals succumbs to disease, predation, or some other mortality factor. Brant live to be quite old; banding data indicate that birds live up to 22 years in the wild.

Pacific brant nest in the high arctic of Alaska, Canada, and Russia. The principal breeding area lies in the great waterfowl production region of the Yukon-Kuskokwim Delta in western Alaska. One estimate of 35,000 to 40,000 pairs suggests that at least half the breeding birds in the population nest there. The north slope of Alaska is also im-

portant, with several thousand pairs present. In Canada, black brant breed on the Mackenzie River Delta, Banks Island, Victoria Island, and Queen Maud Gulf. Additionally, some breeding occurs in Russia on the northern coast of Siberia and Wrangel Island.

Atlantic brant have the distinction of breeding farther north than most other waterfowl. Important breeding grounds are in the high arctic of Canada from Prince Patrick Island in the west to Southampton Island in the south, and east to the coast of Greenland. In the central portion of the Canadian arctic, the breeding range of the Atlantic race overlaps that of the Pacific.

Brant arrive on the breeding grounds in late May or early June. Like other arctic nesting geese, the amount of snow and ice present when they arrive is the single most important factor in determining breeding success. Upon arrival, they must have some snow-free ground to make their nest on and lay eggs. If they are greeted by a blanket of snow and ice, they can only afford to wait a limited time before it's too late to breed for that year.

If the female cannot lay her clutch at the right time, or within a few days of it, she begins to resorb eggs. The longer the wait for the snow to clear, the greater the number of eggs resorbed. If the wait is more than two or three weeks, egg laying will not occur and complete breeding failure can result. This strategy, while devastating on annual reproduction, enhances the long-term survival of the species.

Brant nest in small, loose colonies near tidal sloughs, rivers, or channels. The nest site is often on a small island or promontory extending into a pond or lake. The nest is a bowl-shaped depression or scrape fashioned from fine grasses and lined with down. One waterfowl biologist described the first brant nest he saw as "the most beautiful of all waterfowl nests, with a grass foundation and symmetrical ring of pure down, 14 to 18 inches in diameter. The down was powder-blue, slate, and steel gray forming

an admirable setting for the four or five eggs, which are faintly glossy white or soft ivory" (Clarence Cottam, 1944). The eggs are incubated by the female, and hatch in 23 to 25 days.

Various studies on the Yukon Delta show Pacific brant incubate an average of 3.63 eggs and average 74 percent nest success. In the Anderson River Delta, the clutch size of Atlantic brant averaged slightly larger at 3.92 eggs.

About 24 hours after the slate gray and white goslings hatch, the female leads them to water, and development progresses rapidly. In the land of the midnight sun, the broods are active round-the-clock and spend 18 to 20 hours a day feeding. Both parents are devoted to the care of the brood and will aggressively defend the clan against predators. Predators that pose the most serious threat to both eggs and young are arctic foxes, jaegers, and glaucous gulls. Cold, wet weather during the first two weeks after hatching can also take a heavy toll.

The precocial young grow fast in the arctic and reach flight stage in about 45 days. During the developmental pe-

All species of brant have a small patch of white on the upper neck and a striking white ventral region on an otherwise dark body.

Various angles on the brant provide a good overview of its appearance. On their breeding grounds the brant subsist on sedges and rushes, while in winter they rely heavily on eelgrass. When disease wiped out much of the eelgrass on the Atlantic coast in the 1930s the brant had to either adjust or die. The adjustors learned to eat sea lettuce and various salt-marsh grasses.

riod, the goslings remain in family groups and grow their flight feathers about the same time as the molting adults. Adult birds molt and are flightless for three to four weeks during late July and early August. Non-breeders molt earlier in communal flocks.

MIGRATION

By late August, the family groups have gained strength on the wing and are ready for migration. In late summer, Pacific brant leave the breeding grounds and move south to the Izembek Lagoon on the Alaska Peninsula. At Izembek, they spend September and October feeding on eelgrass in preparation for the fall migration. By late October, virtually the entire world's population of black brant is found there.

In late October or early November, black brant leave Izembek for points south. The departure is spectacular, with more than 100,000 birds present at Izembek Lagoon one day and gone the next. The flocks depart Izembek when the winds aloft are strong and have a south or

A brant strikes a perfect profile. Timid by nature, the brant try to avoid human activity near their watery habitats. In fact, the presence of humans may have led to shifts in their wintering areas.

southeasterly heading. The fall migration, as documented in the 1970s, remains one of nature's most amazing sights.

Similarly, light-bellied brant from the Canadian arctic and Greenland stage at James Bay during September and October. The fall migration of the Atlantic race has not been as well documented, but it is believed that the birds move over land from James Bay to their wintering grounds on the east coast. The wintering grounds are coastal estuaries and bays from Massachusetts to South Carolina. While their distribution encompasses much of the Eastern Seaboard, a high percentage of brant are found along the coast of New Jersey. The second largest wintering population is found on Long Island Sound in New York. Scattered populations winter on the Delaware Bay; along the coast of Maryland and the shores of Chesapeake Bay; Back Bay, Virginia; and on Currituck and Pamlico Sounds

in North Carolina. The January 1997 winter survey showed that 72 percent of the 121,465 Atlantic brant counted were in New Jersey.

During the 1950s, up to 50 percent of the Pacific brant population wintered along the west coast of the United States with the remainder found on the Pacific side of the Baja Peninsula. However, in 1959, while conducting a waterfowl census, biologists with the U.S. Fish and Wildlife Service found more birds wintering in Mexico. At the same time, the number of birds wintering in Washington, Oregon, and California declined. By the late 1960s, not only were there more black brant in Mexico, but they had pioneered new wintering areas along the mainland west coast of Mexico. Today, up to 20 percent of the population migrate to the new Mexican wintering grounds in Sonora and Sinaloa. The remaining birds are found along the

Baja coast at San Quintin Bay, Scammon's Lagoon, San Ignacio Bay, and Magdalena Bay.

Some Pacific brant still winter in the United States, but most birds fly directly from Alaska to Mexico. The only significant wintering populations are in the Puget Sound region of Washington, where up to 20,000 birds are found, along with an increasing number (10,000+) that stay at Izembek Lagoon for the winter. The January 1997 winter survey showed that 83 percent of the 157,905 Pacific brant counted were in Mexico.

An interesting note to the Puget Sound population is that about 50 percent of the birds that winter there are Atlantic brant, while the remainder are Pacific brant. According to the Washington Department of Fish and Wildlife, some of the light-bellied brant that nest on Melville Island in the Canadian arctic fly southwest from their breeding grounds to Washington instead of southeast like the majority of their subspecies.

The reasons for the shift in wintering areas along the Pacific coast have long been a subject of speculation. At the time of the shift, black brant numbers were stable, ruling out a significant change in population levels. Habitat loss was also examined, and while some degradation of eelgrass has occurred, particularly in California, this does not appear to be the problem. More likely, brant, timid by nature, have difficulty tolerating the increased human activity and re-sulting disturbances caused by boaters, fishermen, hunters, clammers, and other bay users, who are particularly active at low tide, when brant obtain most of their food.

In Mexico, the primary wintering areas are secure, and, so far, habitat destruction and human pressures are minimal. Two of the principal wintering areas, Scammon's Lagoon and San Ignacio Bay in Baja, are ecological reserves, where habitat alteration and hunting are prohibited.

While the states along the Pacific coast have diminished in importance as wintering areas, they still play an important role in the annual cycle of Pacific brant. Today, these areas, along with the coast of Vancouver Island, are important spring-use areas during the northward migration to the breeding grounds.

Unlike the fall exodus, spring migration is a gradual affair that takes place between mid-January, when the first birds head north from the wintering grounds, and late May, when they arrive on the breeding grounds. The major advantage to this strategy is that the slow movement allows the adults to build fat reserves for the high energy demands of the breeding season.

I have studied brant from Alaska to Mexico for more than 25 years, and yet each fall when I see my first flock of brant, I remain captivated by their elegant but simple coloration, diminutive size, soft vocalizations, and long-distance migrations.

Canada Goose
(*Branta canadensis*)

BY RICK BURKMAN

Opening pages: A flock of Canada geese fly in a classic V-shaped formation. The sight of these stately birds making their way north or south is an unmistakable sign of seasonal change. *Above:* Active restocking has made the Canada goose a familiar presence—sometimes even a nuisance.

Longing to go where the wild goose goes is one of the strongest symbols of seasonal change. While humans are instinctively stocking their cupboards and settling down for a long winter of cold, blustery days, the gregarious Canada geese are flying southward in their famous lop-sided-vee formations. When we feel the first warm rays of springtime sun on our faces, the geese are already high in the sky, flying to their summer homes. Aldo Leopold, the famous naturalist and author of *The Sand County Almanac*, once wrote, "One swallow does not make a summer, but one skein of geese, cleaving the murk of a March thaw, is spring."

The Canada goose is second only to the mallard in public recognition. Its distinctive black head and neck, white chinstrap, and gray and brown football-shaped body is the subject of artists and cartoonists. Goose caricatures are found on everything from postcards to high school jerseys, from national wildlife refuge signs to living room throw pillows. A giant 24-foot, 3,500-pound goose sculpture honors this well-known waterfowl in the small town of Wawa in Ontario, Canada.

Our admiration for the goose is reflected in our language. Reliable people are "as faithful as a goose." "Sauce for the goose is sauce for the gander" exemplifies fair play, and a person who has earned our admiration through success is "the goose that lays the golden egg." Whether or not we realize it, we revere the goose.

SUCCESSFUL SPECIES

Although abundant and prolific as a species, a few of the 12 recognized Canada goose races have suffered from a combination of hunting pressure and habitat degradation. At one time, the giant form of the species (*Branta canadensis maxima*) was thought to be extinct. It was not officially rediscovered until 1962. Once the large geese were recognized as a missing species, they were reintroduced to game areas and wildlife refuges, starting in the Midwest. The aggressive restocking campaign worked, and the giant

Canada goose is now abundant and familiar. They have been so successful that they are occasionally considered nuisances on some lawns, parks, golf courses, and farm fields.

Canada geese can live for more than 20 years, so there is no great hurry to start a family. Young birds take up to two years to establish pair bonds, and the bonds usually last for life. Reestablishing the pair bond after the birds have been separated takes only a few hours. Even though the pair bonds are strong, they are not absolute. Nest loss to predators or storms may trigger a search for new partners, and paired geese will sometimes split and take new partners for no discernible reason.

Paired birds establish nesting territories near lakes, streams, ponds, or marshes. The nest is built on an elevated platform. Muskrat houses,

Top: The wing lengths of Canada geese can range from 550 millimeters in the giant race to only 330 millimeters in the smallest, the cackling goose. *Above:* The smaller geese tend to travel in larger flocks than do their more sizable relatives.

Above: Large groups of Canada geese can irritate farmers and people who have to clean up after them. *Left:* The geese are powerful fliers with strong wings. *Facing page:* The pair bonds in Canada geese are strong and the parents will actively defend their offspring, as anyone who has encountered a fierce, hissing goose will testify.

the female is off the nest feeding, stretching, or just taking a well-deserved break. After the last egg is laid, the female begins incubating the clutch while the male patrols nearby.

After 28 days, the goslings crack their shells and take their first look at the vast outer world. Tawny, wet, and feeble, the newly hatched birds dry quickly and rapidly gain muscle control and strength. Several hours later, they leave the nest, never looking back. Goslings are natural swimmers that instinctively follow the male parent in single file. The mother guards the rear, protecting the brood and ensuring that the goslings do not stray far from their path.

Canada goose parents are aggressive protectors of their precious offspring. Strong, outstretched wings and wide-open, hissing beaks are overt

beaver lodges, or small islands rising from the water are all common nest sites. Some birds have even nested on rocky cliff sides and, on rare occasions, in abandoned eagle or hawk nests.

Females use mud and nearby vegetation to construct their nests. As material is added to the nest, the goose sits and wiggles in the soft mud, form-ing a depression in which to fit her body. Once satisfied with the nest, she begins laying eggs. One dull white egg is laid each day until a clutch of five or six eggs is complete. Eggs do not stay white for long. Mud, vegetation, and nutrients suspended in the water quickly stain the eggs. The stains then provide camouflage for the eggs while

Atlantic Canada Goose Measurements

	Adult Male	Adult Female	Immature Male	Immature Female
Wing	466.3 mm	465.0 mm		
Weight	8.8 lbs.	7.6 lbs.	7.5 lb.s	6.8 lbs.

Giant Canada Goose Measurements

	Adult Male	Adult Female	Immature Male	Immature Female
Wing	525.8 mm	495.6 mm	498.6 mm	478.3 mm
Weight	12.5 lbs.	11.1 lbs.	10.6 lbs.	8.9 lbs.

Cackling Canada Goose Measurements

	Adult Male	Adult Female
Wing	363.8 mm	353.5 mm
Weight	3.4 lbs.	2.8 lbs.

Western Canada Goose Measurements

	Adult Male	Adult Female
Length	37.1 in.	34.5 in.
Wing	518 mm	478 mm
Weight	9.9 lbs.	8.2 lbs.

threat displays that effectively deter many predators. However, young birds still live in a dangerous world. Ospreys, eagles, and gulls swoop from above to snatch unsuspecting goslings from the water's surface. Snapping turtles and northern pike hunt the downy birds from below. But the natural world always provides a balance and while some goslings are destroyed, others survive to pass their genes on to another generation.

After about six weeks (longer for the larger races), the goslings have changed from peeping bundles of fuzz to fully fledged birds that resemble adults save for an occasional tuft of juvenile fluff sticking out between the stiff mature feathers. Even though the goslings no longer rely on their parents for survival, the family ties remain strong and the group stays together until autumn, when they join other families to form large migrating flocks.

The white chin strap is the Canada goose's most distinctive feature while the long, graceful neck has an almost dinosaurian look to it. The goose will keep its head up in its normal swimming posture but will lower and push it forward when feeling aggressive.

A Canada goose strikes a reflective pose. The geese are popular subjects for carvers and have been for years, with many striking antique goose decoys available for collectors.

The urge to migrate seems stronger in some geese than in others, and many birds move only as far south as needed to find open water. Some winter through the snow and sub-freezing temperatures as long as open water and adequate food exist.

A VARIETY OF RACES

Canada geese are unique in their racial size differences. The largest race, the giant Canada goose, may be as much as seven times larger than the smallest race, known as the cackling goose (*Branta Canadensis minima*). Cackling geese are a little larger than mallards.

In general, Canada geese get smaller from east to west across the North American continent. Although there is a dramatic size difference between widely separated races, intermingling between nearby groups is common, making the change from the largest to the smallest groups a gradual shift rather than an abrupt break. Adding to the confusion is the sexual dichotomy within each race. Males are usually larger than females.

There are currently 12 accepted races of Canada geese. Easily recognizable field marks, including their black heads and necks, white chinstraps and dusky brown bodies, make general identification easy. Some races also sport small white neck rings that act as a visual dividing line between the neck and body. Their breasts are dirty white, flanks buffy brown, and upper parts medium brown with paler feather fringes. Parts of the back, rump, and tail are black. The ventral region and upper-tail coverts are white, and the wing coverts are brown with pale fringes. The primary feathers and underwings are brown and their bills, legs, and feet are deep black.

Even though the general field marks are similar, specific racial changes are evident over large distances. Western birds have relatively smaller bills and shorter necks than the larger eastern races. They are darker and tinted with rich, earthy, reddish-brown hues. The eastern races outmass the smaller subgroups, weighing up to a hefty 20 pounds, and have proportionately longer wingspans, occasionally as wide as a staggering 75 inches.

On close examination, it is evident that the body morphology of the different races also varies greatly. Large races have legs positioned forward on their bodies, shifting their centers of gravity to the central part of their bodies and over their strong legs.

Many people have studied the habits of the Canada goose. Their migration routes, foods and habitat preferences are all well documented. But there is still a sense of wonder and awe that makes our hearts swell with exultation when we see a skein high up in a leaden sky. They are a sure sign that the seasons are swiftly marching past and the mystery of change is once again upon us. It is little wonder that we long to go where the wild goose goes.

Common Loon
(Gavia immer)

BY JEROME A. JACKSON

Opening pages: **A common loon swims with its young. Loons often carry their chicks on their backs to protect them from underwater predators.** *Above:* **The loons' legs are located so far back on their bodies they have difficulty moving about on land. This restricts them to the water and shore very close to the water's edge.**

A foggy spring morning at sunrise, wood smoke mixed with the scent of northern conifers, a placid lake, and just a bit of a chill in the air. What's missing? Listen. The haunting call of the common loon provides the capping touch, the wild spirit of the scene. Perhaps it was the movie *On Golden Pond* that fixed this image in the collective mind of the American public, but it is a real image that has been appreciated by humans for millennia. The common loon, with its seemingly maniacal calls, its stunning plumage, its grace in the water, its powerful flight, has been the subject of legend, folklore, and wonder for all who have known it. It is the state bird of Minnesota, the provincial bird of Ontario, and is featured on the Canadian dollar coin affectionately known as the "loony."

Loons are strictly northern hemisphere birds. Although there are five species, all are similar in form, behavior, and ecology, such that each is readily recognizable by its "loonness." Although we generally think of loons as being birds of the far north, in truth they spend as much or more time in southern wintering areas. Young common loons re-main in the south, at least through their first year. Adult common loons molt their flight feathers all at once in late winter and, for the few weeks it takes for new ones to grow in, they are flightless.

The loon we will focus on here is the most common and best known in North America, which is why we call it the common loon. This bird is found through much of the northern hemisphere, nesting on both sides of the Atlantic. In Great Britain, it is known as the "great northern diver," a name that tells us a bit more about the bird: it is the largest of the loon species, and it captures its food by diving for it.

A loon is a fisherman, and is among the most proficient of all diving birds. Although most of its fishing is done in relatively shallow water, some loons have been captured in fishing nets at depths of as much as 240 feet. A loon can also swim great distances underwater in pursuit of prey, although it generally stays underwater for little more than a minute. A loon has many adaptations that make it particularly efficient at doing this, and these adaptations also impose limits on its other activities. To best accomplish and present a carving of a loon, it is important that the carver understand these unique adaptations.

THE ANATOMY OF A LOON

All of our loons have distinct breeding, wintering, and juvenile plumages. The wintering and juvenile plumages of the common loon are relatively dull and lack the spotting and necklace that characterize the species. In John James Audubon's portrait of two common loons, he includes one bird in breeding plumage and the other in winter. Some have misinterpreted the painting to be showing a bright male and his duller mate; in truth, the sexes have the same plumages, the male differing only in being very slightly larger. While loons in all except the downy natal plumages can be found on the birds' Gulf and southern Atlantic coast wintering grounds, on northern lakes adults are almost always in the beautiful breeding plumage that I will emphasize here.

A loon is long-bodied, superbly contoured to slip through the water like a torpedo in search of its prey. It

The loon's necklace and throat patch are made up of tiny feathers, each of which is white with a black streak down the center. The loon's necklace is broken by solid gaps of about 20 millimeters in front and six to eight millimeters in back.

Common Loon Measurements*	Adult Average
Length from the black on the front of the neck to the tip of the tail	520 mm
Wing from the wrist of the folded wing to the tip of the longest primary feather	340 mm
Tail from between the base of the two central tail feathers to the tip of the longest of those tail feathers	110 mm
Length of the upper bill from the base along the top	83 mm

* From *Wildfowl Carving Magazine*, Spring 1999

A loon's bill is shiny black, shading almost imperceptibly to a horn gray near the tip. It is long and sharply pointed for use as delicate pincers in preening, feeding young, and manipulating prey. Newly hatched chicks are black except for a white belly.

is also moderately long-necked, giving the diving bird the facility to reach quickly a few inches to the right or left to grab evasive prey. Its legs are positioned far back on the body and splayed somewhat—extending outward and behind the swimming bird, rather than under it. As a result, a loon can't stand up and walk as other birds do. A loon is essentially restricted to a life on the water or in the air, struggling ashore only to nest at the water's edge. If lake levels fall after a loon has begun nesting, it must push itself on its belly, with great effort, to reach the nest.

Close examination of a loon's legs and feet reveals further structural specialization for swimming. Most birds have legs and toes that are more or less round or oval in cross section; not so with a loon. A loon's legs and toes are incredibly flattened, allowing it to slice through the water with ease and minimal drag. Its toes are very long, the longest being slightly longer than the tarsus. The first bone of each toe is the longest, more than twice the length of the other toe bones, and the three forward facing toes are linked by a strikingly black-and-white web.

A loon's wings are small relative to its body size, and narrow. But the wing feathers are strong, and the breast muscles used in flight are large and powerful. The small wings are an important adaptation in that they create minimal drag as they are clasped tightly against the loon's sides during dives. They are not used during dives except to help stabilize the bird and occasionally help it steer during a sharp turn. Perhaps an indication of their importance to a loon are the limits placed on a loon as a result of its small wings: to take off, a common loon needs a running start. It can't just leap from the water as a mallard does, but rather it must begin its takeoff by swimming rapidly on the surface, flapping its wings, and then literally running across the surface of the water for 20 yards or more in order to get airborne. Once in the air, it must continue to beat its wings rapidly, but can attain a flight speed of more than 60 (sometimes more than 80) miles per hour. When coming in to land, because of its small wings and heavy weight, a loon must come in fast, sometimes splashing down in a rather ungainly fashion. These limits to its flight mean that a loon is limited to large bodies of water—like a jet plane that requires an extra-long runway, it must have ample room for takeoff. A loon that lingers too late on a northern lake sometimes faces the real threat of being trapped if too much of the lake freezes overnight, reducing the requisite expanse of open water for takeoff.

A loon's eyes are deep red, a color also found in many other diving birds. The significance of this color is not certain, but it may enhance the bird's vision at depths reached by only certain wavelengths of light from above. A loon's bill is shiny black, shading almost imperceptibly near the tip to a horn gray. It is long and sharply pointed for use as delicate pincers in preening, feeding young, and manipulating prey—not for spearing its prey. On the other hand, the bill can also be used defensively and is a formidable weapon. In 1899, a man was killed when stabbed by the bill of a wounded loon! The cutting edge of the upper bill is slightly concave on many specimens, providing the loon with a bill that is somewhat contoured for gripping and holding onto a fish. A loon's nostrils are about 10 mm long, slit-like and very close to the feathers of the face.

PLUMAGE

The common loon's head and neck are velvety black, with a slight touch of iridescent green on the back of the head and neck, shading to an iridescent greenish purple on the sides and lower throat. The loon's necklace and throat patch, the subjects of Native American legends as to their origin, are made up of tiny feathers, each of which is white with a black streak down the center. The loon's necklace is broken by solid black gaps of about 20 millimeters in front and six to eight millimeters in back. The necklace is widest on the sides and back and tapers noticeably toward the front. Although the necklace can be as much as 32 to 35 millimeters wide when the neck is outstretched, the width decreases when the neck is not extended. In normal swimming posture, a loon's neck is held in a graceful S-shape, with its bill held nearly level. The closely related yellow-billed loon, in contrast, tends to hold its bill oriented slightly upward.

A loon's body is well counter-shaded: dark above and light below. Fishes looking up at a swimming loon may not see it because its white belly is camouflaged against the light sky. Similarly, a predator or fish looking at a loon from above may miss it because its dark, white-spotted back blends in with the dark lake or stream bottom and the dappling of light on the water surface. Just how important is countershading to the common loon? It must be

Loon chicks generally come in pairs. They are capable of swimming within a day of hatching although at first they are so buoyant they have difficulty diving.

very important in allowing the bird to get close enough to capture its prey, since the intricacies of the pattern of light above/dark below extend beyond that normally found in birds. The loon's legs, feet and even its long, very flattened toenails have a contrasting black-and-white countershading pattern! Holding a live loon in my arms, I immediately saw that the countershading appeared to be backward. It's the top of the bird's foot that is white (with some black) and the bottom that is black (with some white). But on considering how the loon uses its legs and feet while swimming, the pattern becomes clear.

When swimming, the loon's legs extend straight behind it such that the bottom of the foot is facing upward and the top is facing downward.

Although the visual effect of the loon's color pattern may be artistically rendered in different ways, the final result will be most convincing if you understand the pattern as it occurs on individual feathers. The streaking on the common loon's sides and flanks is made up of feathers that have a black center stripe or ones that have markings that form somewhat of a diffuse W near the feather tip. The W is darkest (brownish black), tallest and widest at the cen-

ter peak, which includes the stiff shaft of the feather. On the breast and flanks, the streaking is heaviest close to the back and becomes finer and finer where it extends into the white of the breast and belly.

The dappled pattern on the loon's back is similarly a function of the pattern on individual feathers. Each of the contour feathers on the loon's back has a single white spot in each web a few millimeters back from the tip. The pattern begins as tiny white spots (about one millimeter in diameter) just behind the neck, increasing gradually to larger white rectangular (six by eight millimeter) markings on the back. On the lower back and rump, the spots abruptly become small again, increasing slightly in size on the upper- (and under-) tail coverts such that they remind me of the spotting on a guinea fowl.

White spots on the wing also show a gradient in size from small at the leading edge and shoulder of the wing to larger toward the back of the wing.

Spots along the side of the body below where the wing is held at rest match and are lined up with those of the back of the wing, resulting in the folded wing blending into the body very well.

The tail of a loon is relatively short and stiff, comprised of brownish black feathers with no iridescence. It is unusual in that the number of rectrices (true tail feathers) seems to vary from 16 to 20. This variation may not be real, but instead a reflection of the difficulty of superficially distinguishing rectrices from upper-tail coverts. These coverts, which on most birds are small and simply cover the gaps between rectrices, are nearly as long as the rectrices, essentially making the tail a multi-layered, stiff, horizontal rudder that facilitates pursuit of prey underwater. The rectrices extend three to five millimeters beyond the tips of the coverts and, unlike the coverts, have a narrow band of white at the rounded tips. Among the specimens I examined, some had the white tips so

Above: The loon has relatively small wings and the birds require a long running start across the surface of the water before they can lumber into the air. Once airborne, though, they are fast fliers. *Right:* The loon's eye is a striking red. The reason for this evolutionary development remains a mystery but it probably has something to do with the loon's need to see well in the dark depths.

worn that the tips only appeared slightly lighter than the rest of the feather; birds in fresher plumage had a white band about two millimeters wide.

Among poses that a carver might want to consider would be a loon asleep. Although loons typically sleep afloat on the water, where they are safest from predators, an incubating loon also sleeps on the nest. In either location, a loon sleeps with its head turned and bill buried in the feathers of its upper back. In this position, it breathes the warm air trapped beneath the feathers. Another pose you might consider would be that of a swimming loon with a downy chick on its back. Newly hatched chicks are sooty black except for a white belly. By climbing onto a parent's back, a downy chick gains safety from large fish and snapping turtles, and conserves energy that would otherwise be lost through its feet in cold water or expended in swimming.

ENVIRONMENTAL CONCERNS

Although the loon is a well-known and well-loved bird, in recent decades, loon numbers and the areas occupied by nesting loons have declined. Pesticides have taken some toll, but so, too, have acid rain, discarded monofilament fishing line, lead from fishing weights, oil spills, mercury, and other pollutants. Perhaps the most serious continuing threats for loons are human intrusion in nesting areas and disregard for their habitat needs. Motor boats and jet skis are serious problems because they generate waves and

The streaking on the loon's sides and flanks is made up of feathers that have a black center stripe or ones that form a somewhat diffuse W near the feather tips.

The male and female common loon look alike—this bird is in winter plumage, which is much less distinctive than the better-known summer coloring.

disturbances that can cause nest abandonment and separate chicks from their parents. Curious canoeists, picnickers, and photographers who can't resist a "closer look" also take a toll on loons, causing abandoned nests and making chicks and eggs more vulnerable to predators.

There are some positive developments relative to loons, too. Use of lead fishing weights has been prohibited in some areas. "Loon Rangers" monitor nests from a distance and steer others clear of nesting areas. Floating nest platforms have been developed that loons readily use. These are a useful management tool where predators and people around the shores of a lake are a serious threat. They are also important where lake water levels fluctuate greatly as a result of irregular and excessive releases of water from behind dams. People are learning about the needs of loons, and there are many local and regional loon conservation groups, many of which are affiliated with the North American Loon Fund.

Pied-billed Grebe
(Podilymbus podiceps)

BY JEROME A. JACKSON

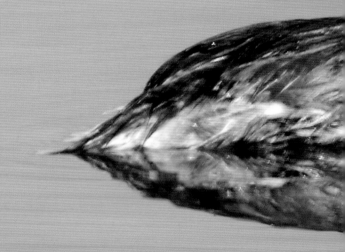

Opening pages: If it walks like a duck and quacks like a duck, then it's a duck. The pied-billed grebe is not a duck. *Above:* The pointed bill and small tail are two features that separate the grebe from ducks. The feet are different, too, with lobes instead of webs.

"It moved! It's gone!" While pushing my canoe through an opening in a stand of cattails, buttonbushes, and grasses in shallow water at Noxubee National Wildlife Refuge in Mississippi, I spotted a curious brown clump half-hidden by weeds. I didn't see the animal sitting on it, but then it moved, and I caught a glimpse as it slipped quickly from the mound and beneath the water's surface. What was it? I waited, but it didn't surface. I went to the clump to look for evidence left behind. A muskrat, I thought. Then I discovered the seven elongate, pale, some-what chalky, blue-white eggs—my first nest of a "water witch," the pied-billed grebe.

What's a grebe? Scientists would like the answer to that one. There are at least 20 species of grebes found around the world. All are birds incredibly adapted to aquatic environments. They're not closely related to ducks. A grebe's bill is narrow and pointed, not broad and flattened. Grebes are not closely related to loons, either. Some studies suggest they are distant relatives of herons and storks, but, clearly, grebes diverged from their nearest kin millions of years ago. Unlike ducks, loons, herons, storks, and their

relatives, a grebe's feet are lobed, not webbed. There are more different grebes in the New World than anywhere else, and the pied-billed grebe is found over a greater range than any other grebe species.

Although migrant where waters freeze over in winter, the pied-billed grebe returns to those areas almost as soon as they become ice-free in spring and departs only shortly before ponds ice over in winter. It nests where there is emergent vegetation in ponds and lakes, and along slow streams through most of the United States, southern Canada, and south through Central America and the West Indies and all but the southern tip of South America. The pied-billed grebe also nests in Hawaii, and a few have made it to Europe.

The accepted common name, "pied-billed," comes from its short, stout, chicken-like bill that, in the breeding season, has a prominent black band that rings it. Except for the band, the bill appears bluish-white with a darker ridge on the curved upper bill. In winter, the bill is more horn-colored and the black bill band is missing. The legs and feet of the pied-billed grebe are lead gray to black.

Audubon called this bird the "pied-billed dob-chick," a corruption of the name "dabchick," which today refers to a European grebe. Colloquial names for the pied-billed grebe include "diedapper," "dabchick," "hell-diver," and "water witch," most of which refer to its ability to disappear by silently sinking into the water while hardly leaving a ripple on the surface. Another name, "*sac-a-plomb*," used by early French Americans, really sums it up: "sack of lead." Like a sack of lead, a pied-billed grebe can sink out of sight!

PLUMAGE

The pied-billed grebe is a stocky bird with a small head that blends in with its thick neck to give the partially submerged bird an almost snake-like appearance. It appears to be tailless, but does have short, non-descript tail feathers. The sexes of pied-billed grebes are indistinguishable by plumage and their sizes overlap, although males average slightly larger than females. In breeding plumage, the whitish bill is continuous, and a thin, white ring surrounds the eye. Adults have a forehead covered with brownish-black feathers that are stiff and somewhat bristle-like. Much of the grebe's body plumage is very silky in texture.

The dark forehead shades to a slightly lighter brown on the crown and more distinctly to gray-buff on the nape, cheeks, and lower neck. The relatively uniform color of the neck gives way to an incredibly dense patch of feathers that are almost white at the base, change to dark brown at their widest point, and are tipped in white to buff. The effect on the living grebe is somewhat of an earthy mosaic. Feathers of the lower breast and central belly seem whitest because the light feather tips are longer and lighter. Feathers to the edge of the breast and toward the rump appear darker and duller buff, lacking most of the light tip. Buff flanks are subtly barred to

On the water the grebe looks like a cross between a chicken and a sea serpent. Its ability to slip beneath the surface without a trace earned it the nicknames "water witch" and "*sac-a-plomb*," French for "sack of lead."

Pied-billed Grebe Measurements*	Adult Male	Adult Female
Length	31–38 cm	31–38 cm
Wing Chord	124–145 mm	112–131 mm
Exposed Culmen	20–24 mm	17–21 mm

* From *Wildfowl Carving Magazine*, Summer 2001

blotched with dark brown blending with a silvery white near the base of individual feathers. Neck, breast, and belly feathers are dense, soft, and lustrous. The soft feathers under the tail are distinctly white. When viewed from behind, the white rump of the grebe is very evident. A pied-billed grebe's back, wings, and upper tail are dark brown, shading somewhat to olive and, when fresh, to light tips on some feathers, giving the plumage a slightly "frosted" appearance.

The breeding pied-billed grebe's characteristic black throat patch extends about 4 cm from the lower bill onto the neck. At its widest, it is about 1.5 cm across. The tiny feathers bordering the sides of the throat patch are whitish, and are lightest near the bill, fading into the gray-buff cheek and neck. Examination of specimens reveals that the white border is more distinct in some males. On juveniles and winter adults, the black throat patch is replaced by a whitish to buff patch that is whitest at the throat and grades into the gray-buff of the neck.

DAILY LIFE

Pied-billed grebes are not nearly as social as other grebe species, although in winter half a dozen grebes are occasionally seen in a loose group, and hundreds can be found in some migratory staging areas. The generally solitary life of pied-billed grebes may explain why their courtship lacks much of the razzle-dazzle of other grebe species. There are no spectacular ritualized aquatic ballets or upright races of birds across the surface of the water, such as we see in some other grebes. Pair members will sometimes share spring duets. These can include a lengthy vocal performance that begins with low "wup" notes followed by a series of "kow" notes that are at first soft and slow, and then increase in volume and tempo, and sometimes end with an alternating series of drawn-out "kowoo" notes and gulping "gow"

Top: Pied-billed grebe chicks take to the water within 24 hours. Like loons, they will often ride on their parents' backs, even underwater. *Above:* When in breeding plumage, the adult grebe sports a distinctive black throat patch.

The black band on the grebe's bill makes it "pied," a word more commonly associated with patterned horses. The satiny breast feathers were once in great demand for fashionable accessories such as turbans and muffs.

notes. The performance is a spring spectacular that echoes through the cattails that often hide the performers.

A pied-billed grebe's nest is linked to the bird's highly aquatic nature. It is a mass of decaying vegetation brought up from the bottom and placed in shallow water. Sometimes it is built up from the bottom. At other times, it floats, secured loosely to emergent plants so that it can gently rise and fall with water levels. The nest site is often near emergent vegetation, but also has at least one stretch of open water that allows the grebes to approach their nest underwater. Most nesting takes place in freshwater ponds. Although the pied-billed grebe occasionally nests in salt marshes, it does so only where tidal changes are minimal. Any considerable tide fluctuation would likely result in nest destruction.

Where the climate allows, pied-billed grebes have a long nesting season, producing two and, in the south, perhaps even three broods per year. As incubation proceeds, eggs become more polished and are often stained with brown from the decaying plants in their nest. When a parent leaves the nest, it usually covers the eggs with vegetation, hiding them from predators and the hot sun.

Downy black and with a white pin-striped head pattern, pied-billed grebe chicks hatch after an incubation period of about 23 days. They leave the nest within 24 hours and are at home swimming, although they readily seek safety and a ride by climbing onto a parent's back. At times, an adult will sink out of sight, leaving chicks bobbing on the surface. At other times, the young will continue their ride underwater, tucked into their parent's back feathers. While adults have relatively few aquatic predators, chicks are prime prey for larger fish and turtles. Thus, the ride on a parent's back is often the key to survival.

At the nest, the pair share the domestic duties of nest building, incubation, and care of young. Females often seem to do more of the incubation. When grebes exchange positions at the nest, they gently touch bill tips in a simple ritual. Such caresses, however, are reserved for a mate and chicks. The pied-billed grebe is a feisty bird that readily attacks neighboring grebes and other birds. And, like a prankster at a swimming hole, its favorite mode of attack is from below.

No bird seems more at ease in its aquatic environment than the pied-billed grebe. Within its wet medium, its movements are subtly smooth—first you see it, then you don't. These grebes are wary skulkers! With the approach of potential danger, a grebe exhales and compresses its plumage to release trapped air, then sinks out of sight leaving hardly a ripple on the surface. When surprised, a pied-billed grebe's dive can be a forceful plunge forward that can send a spray of water two meters into the air. Underwater, a pied-billed grebe is fast and agile, depending almost exclusively on its strong legs and toes for propulsion and maneuvering, and only rarely using its wings as it makes sharp turns in pursuit of prey.

A pied-billed grebe in search of food makes repeated dives. Most begin with a smooth, short leap forward and last for 10 to 30 seconds. The diet of a pied-billed grebe is diverse and opportunistic, including an array of small fish, amphibians, crustaceans, insect larvae, snails, and other invertebrates. The heavy bill of the pied-billed grebe is thought to be an adaptation for dealing with the hard bodies of the insects, crayfish, and other arthropods that it eats. Numerically, nearly half of this grebe's prey species are insects and a third are crustaceans. Most of these are probably slower and easier to capture than fish, which comprise about 20 percent of their prey.

Among the more curious and abundant items consistently found in the stomachs of pied-billed grebes are grebe feathers. Audubon discovered that these birds eat their own feathers. Others have found that grebes feed their feathers to their chicks. The significance of this behavior may be that the feathers safely trap fish bones, preventing injury to the bird and allowing for the bones to be digested or regurgitated.

ANATOMY

To achieve agility and speed underwater, a grebe's legs are placed far back on its body. The position of the pied-billed grebe's legs is also often accentuated by a resting posture it sometimes assumes in the water, in which its body seems to be rolled slightly to one side such that one foot is raised and appears to be coming from the bird's rump. The Latin name for the family of grebes, Podicipedidae, and the species name *podiceps* for the pied-billed grebe literally mean "rump-foot," and one of the local names for one of the European grebes, "arsefoot," also picks up on this anatomical peculiarity.

So far back are a grebe's legs that it is very awkward on land. Unable to stand upright, it scoots along, pushing with its legs and lobed feet and pulling to some extent with its wings. When resting on land, it is either on the breast or precariously balanced on the tail and tarsi. But the mobility it lacks on land is more than made up for in the water. The pied-billed grebe's tarsi are flattened so that they cut through the water, knife-like, thus minimizing energy ex-

The grebe's pied bill is well adapted for its diet of hard-bodied crustaceans and insects. Grebes also like to dine on fish, when they can catch them, and amphibians.

Above: The throat patch and the band on the bill are characteristic of the grebe's breeding plumage. *Right:* Those two features disappear when the bird reverts to its somewhat drabber winter plumage.

penditure as the tarsi are drawn forward prior to each powerful thrust. Its legs are also capable of rotating more than those of other birds, providing the grebe with incredible agility.

The nails on a pied-billed grebe's broadly lobed toes are unusual in that they are flat like a fingernail, rather than claw-like. On a specimen I measured, the outer two toes on each foot were about 56 mm long, whereas the inner toe was about 43 mm, and the hind toe (which is raised about 5 mm above the others) was only 12 mm long. The flat tarsus has scales that give it a peculiar serrated look along the trailing edge.

Other grebe adaptations for its watery world include its dense, satiny plumage, which insulates it from cold and streamlines it for speed. The pied-billed's mud-brown back allows it to blend in from above whether swimming or sitting on its nest, while its silvery gray breast camouflages it against the light sky when viewed from below. A pied-billed grebe's brownish-red eyes also contribute to its success; the red increases visual acuity in murky water.

The flight of pied-billed grebes is an enigma to me. Short wings add to a grebe's aquatic agility at the expense of aerial prowess. Although I love this bird and have known it well for more than 40 years, I can recall only twice

The grebe's nest is a mass of decaying vegetation brought up from the bottom and placed in shallow water. Loosely secured to emergent plants, it can rise and fall with water levels. The male and female grebes will share the duties of building the next, incubating the eggs, and taking care of the young, although the females seem to do most of the incubation.

that I have seen one fly! With short, stubby wings and a relatively heavy body, these grebes must run across the surface of the water to take off. Once in flight, they must beat their wings rapidly and maintain a relatively direct course.

While northern populations of pied-billed grebes are highly migratory, their migration seems to be done exclusively at night. During migration they take off after dark and then, just before dawn, find a suitable pond for feeding and resting during the day. On rainy nights during migration, the search for a pond to land in for the day is sometimes disastrous. Pied-billed grebes spy their ponds from some altitude and dive into them rather than coming in for a soft landing. They seem unable to distinguish between a lighted wet asphalt parking lot and a pond surface. With great regularity, during both spring and fall migrations, I have found dead pied-billed grebes that have crashed into asphalt parking lots, roads, and even flat roofs.

CONSERVATION

In the late 1800s and early 1900s, pied-billed and other grebes had a price on their heads. Their close-plumed, satiny silver breasts were sought for use on turbans, muffs, and capes. At the same time, their numbers were declining as a result of efforts to drain wetlands to convert marshlands to farmlands. They were also shot indiscriminately. Considered inedible, they were often shot simply for sport.

Protective laws and an end to the feather trade ended most shooting of grebes.

Although the pied-billed grebe made a comeback from the hunting of a century ago, it is once again on the decline. It disappeared as a breeding bird from Rhode Island sometime after the 1950s, and has been listed as endangered in Connecticut, New Hampshire, and New Jersey. Recent declines are probably the result of habitat destruction in wintering, migratory stopover, and breeding areas, as well as disturbance of breeding birds by boaters. Pied-billed grebes are also vulnerable to oil pollution, entanglement in plastic six-pack wrappers and monofilament fishing lines, capture in fishing nets, and collision with guy wires on tall communication towers (during nocturnal migration).

So, what are the challenges of carving the water witch? There are several. First is the challenge of being able to observe one to learn postures and get a good feel for its persona without it suddenly disappearing. A second is dealing with the rich, earthy subtleties of the colors and patterns of its plumage—varying shades and patterns of buff, brown, gray, and white. Then there is the challenge of capturing grebe textures: the silkiness of its breast and the scale patterns on its legs and lobed feet. The ultimate challenge is to capture its on-again-off-again buoyancy and feisty temperament in the context of its watery world.